CultureShock!
A Survival Guide to Customs and Etiquette

Bahrain

Harvey Tripp
Margaret Tripp

Marshall Cavendish
Editions

This edition published in 2008 by:
Marshall Cavendish Corporation
99 White Plains Road
Tarrytown, NY 10591-9001
www.marshallcavendish.us

Other Marshall Cavendish Offices:
Marshall Cavendish International (Asia) Private Limited. 1 New Industrial Road,
Singapore 536196 ■ Marshall Cavendish Ltd. 5th Floor, 32–38 Saffron Hill,
London EC1N 8FH, UK ■ Marshall Cavendish International (Thailand) Co Ltd.
253 Asoke, 12th Flr, Sukhumvit 21 Road, Klongtoey Nua, Wattana, Bangkok
10110, Thailand ■ Marshall Cavendish (Malaysia) Sdn Bhd, Times Subang,
Lot 46, Subang Hi-Tech Industrial Park, Batu Tiga, 40000 Shah Alam, Selangor
Darul Ehsan, Malaysia

Marshall Cavendish is a trademark of Times Publishing Limited

ISBN 10: 0-7614-5473-X
ISBN 13: 978-0-7614-5473-1

Please contact the publisher for the Library of Congress catalog number

Printed in China by Everbest Printing Co Ltd

ABOUT THE SERIES

Culture shock is a state of disorientation that can come over anyone who has been thrust into unknown surroundings, away from one's comfort zone. *CultureShock!* is a series of trusted and reputed guides which has, for decades, been helping expatriates and long-term visitors to cushion the impact of culture shock whenever they move to a new country.

Written by people who have lived in the country and experienced culture shock themselves, the authors share all the information necessary for anyone to cope with these feelings of disorientation more effectively. The guides are written in a style that is easy to read and covers a range of topics that will arm readers with enough advice, hints and tips to make their lives as normal as possible again.

Each book is structured in the same manner. It begins with the first impressions that visitors will have of that city or country. To understand a culture, one must first understand the people—where they came from, who they are, the values and traditions they live by, as well as their customs and etiquette. This is covered in the first half of the book.

Then on with the practical aspects—how to settle in with the greatest of ease. Authors walk readers through how to find accommodation, get the utilities and telecommunications up and running, enrol the children in school and keep in the pink of health. But that's not all. Once the essentials are out of the way, venture out and try the food, enjoy more of the culture and travel to other areas. Then be immersed in the language of the country before discovering more about the business side of things.

To round off, snippets of basic information are offered before readers are 'tested' on customs and etiquette of the country. Useful words and phrases, a comprehensive resource guide and list of books for further research are also included for easy reference.

CONTENTS

Chapter 8
Learning Arabic 123

Chapter 9
Doing Business in Bahrain 129

Chapter 10
Bahrain at a Glance 160

FOREWORD

Bahrain—the world's smallest desert kingdom, yet immensely rich in culture and history. Bahrain's history was born in the ancient world. Now a liberal Islamic society, Bahrain is one of the few Middle Eastern places where churches are a stone's throw away from mosques. If you are worshipping in the Anglican Cathedral in Bahrain, Muslims prayers will be within earshot. The country's liberal attitudes are a result of an ever-evolving economy that was first based on pearls, then oil, and now on banking and finance. Bahrainis boast of a long exposure to trading with foreigners and a lot of interaction with a significant expatriate community in the heart of their homeland. Bahrain caters to the needs of its significant cosmopolitan society. English is widely spoken and there is a good standard of accommodation for visitors and residents.

We have written this book as we see Bahrain now, but there is nothing so constant as change. One of the authors grew up in Bahrain and we have both made many visits as adults for business or business-related reasons while observing the changes over time. Our aim is to give you an objective view on what's good about Bahrain, what's not so good and how to adjust to the culture shock. The book has primarily been written from a Western perspective for English-speaking visitors. It contains background information on historical events, providing the reader with an insight as to how Bahrainis have evolved their unique culture, appearing to be the same as other Arabs in the Arabian Gulf.

This book is also a guide to customs and etiquette of Bahrain. There are no absolute binding rules, other than to remember that the visitor is a guest in Bahrain and should therefore pay due deference to the host—the Bahrainis. Follow this maxim and you are unlikely to offend.

Our aim includes revealing what Bahrain is really like for the foreigner. We hope that, as a result of reading this book, you will know how to interact with the Bahrainis and what to expect from them. We also hope to tell you what it is like to live as an expatriate in one of the world's smallest kingdoms with a large and diverse foreign community.

ACKNOWLEDGEMENTS vii

With thanks for contributions, advice, and reading the manuscript: John Butler, Nonie Coutts, Neville De Souza, Pati Edwards, Carol Melrose, Peter North, Peter O'Brien, Col Sauvarin, Avril and Rod Taylor, Aubrey Tiedt, Len Tripp, La'ali'A and Abdulrahman Zayyani.

MAP OF BAHRAIN

KING FAHD
CAUSEWAY

MANAMA

BAHRAIN

GULF
OF
BAHRAIN

GULF
OF
BAHRAIN

HAWAR
ISLANDS

FIRST IMPRESSIONS

CHAPTER 1

'Bahrain is by no means a backwater. Behind the high-rise
banks crowded on to an imposing esplanade the older
streets of Manama the capital, retain an unasssuming
colonial ambience, the thoroughfares relatively narrow,
the uniforms not quite British.'
—*Melbourne Herald Sun* Newspaper

MANY FREQUENT INTERNATIONAL TRAVELLERS have touched down at the Bahrain International Airport on the island of Muharraq on a number of occasions when flying from Europe to destinations such as Asia or Australasia. However, many of them are only in transit, and do not venture beyond the airport's duty free store.

The minute you decide to take a business trip or are posted to Bahrain, you will probably have a mental picture of a desert island sheikhdom somewhere in Arabia that is subject to bouts of violence and extreme heat. Perhaps if you are a woman, you may have been told that Bahrain is a male-dominated society and you will be required to wear a veil in public. Others sometimes compare Bahrain with Dubai in the United Arab Emirates (UAE) or Dharan in eastern Saudi Arabia. Those that have actually travelled around the Arabian Gulf may say that Dubai has all the attractions of a city whereas Manama, the capital of Bahrain, is more like a provincial town. Some may comment on how geographically small Bahrain is, and complain that there is nowhere to go, unlike the United Arab Emirates or Oman where there are opportunities to go *wadi* bashing and camping in the desert.

Should you meet an expat family who has lived in Bahrain for a long time, you will be surprised when they comment favourably on how Bahrain has a lot more Arab charm than other Arabian Gulf countries, being a smaller community and

The Ahmad Al Fateh Mosque or Grand Mosque that is open to the public outside prayer times.

friendlier place to live in. You may be even more astonished to know that some expats continue to live in Bahrain after their retirement because of the pleasant lifestyle.

AN ARAB EXCEPTION

As your aircraft makes its approach to Bahrain and as you look out the cabin window, there is the contrast of a cloudless azure sky, the turquoise shallow waters of the Arabian Gulf and a hostile featureless yellow desert that seems to go on forever.

Looking downwards, you may notice oil and gas tankers plying the Arabian Gulf or warships that will probably remind you that this is a region of conflict. This is reinforced as your aircraft taxis into the terminal where you will see a squadron of aircraft from the United States Air Force on the tarmac.

However, your initial fears will probably recede when you greet the first Bahrainis you meet—the friendly and efficient immigration and custom officers. In the arrival lounge, you will notice other Bahrainis, donned with headdresses and long flowing robes—outfits you may not be familiar with—but you will be pleasantly surprised as you realise that many around you are speaking a language you understand—English.

As you walk outdoors, you will be greeted by the noonday heat. With daytime temperatures as high as 40°C (104°C) coupled with high humidity, most are relieved to seek refuge indoors which are air-conditioned most of the time.

The modern landscapes and buildings seem to be an antithesis to the rich traditions still distinct in their Bahraini garb and ubiquitous mosques present in the very heart of the society. The pictures of the king that are on billboards everywhere add to the complex image of Bahrain. But as soon as you start to delve into the culture and everyday life, you will soon gain the impression that Bahrain is not, like another Middle Eastern country, a fabulously oil rich sheikhdom, but an Arab exception.

LAND AND HISTORY OF BAHRAIN

CHAPTER 2

'The island is a pleasant oasis. It is friendly, not
hateful like the abominable coast that faces it—
it is not antagonistic to life and does not breed a
missing link as the littoral Arab... The golden-dusted
roads which cross it are broad and shaded on either side
by long forests of date palms, deepening into an
impenetrable greenness, cool with the sound of wind
among the great leaves and the tinkle of flowing water.'
—Aubrey Herbert writing on Bahrain in 1905

THE BEGINNINGS

Archaelogists claim that there is evidence that Bahrain was the Garden of Eden. They might have said so because the history of Bahrain can be traced back to the beginning of civilisation. Originally part of the Arabian Peninsula, Bahrain only became an island around 6000 BC. International archaeologists have found flint tools evidence of the existence of nomads who travelled over Bahrain's desert about ten thousand years ago.

Later, Bahrain became an important stop on the great historical trade routes because of its famous pearls, agricultural products (especially dates) and fishing. Almost since the dawn of history, Bahrain was a buoyant centre for communication and trade because of its good harbour and plentiful amounts of fresh water.

Dilmun

A Sumerian poet wrote, 'The land of Dilmun is holy, the land of Dilmun is pure.' Even in its own time, Dilmun was regarded as a special place shrouded in legend and myth. Bahrain, according to the Sumerian legend recounted in the *Epic of Gilgamesh*, was the Land of Eternal Youth and Paradise because of its abundance of the two essential elements of life—water and food.

From 4000–2000 BC, Bahrain was the centre of the ancient Dilmun Empire. Bahrain was an important port for the ships sailing around the Arabian Gulf and the Arabian Sea. At the peak of the Dilmun era, around 2250–1800 BC, the major city of Qal'at al-Bahrain had a population of at least 7,000 people. Archaeological finds of stone, seals and pottery in Qatif and Dharan in present day Saudi Arabia, Failaka in present day Kuwait and Umm An Nar in present day UAE indicate strong trading links between Dilmun and these centres. Dilmun also became attractive to pirates because of its abundance of fresh water and its pearls then known as fisheyes.

Qal'at al-Bahrain, the Bahrain Fort, is the most prominent of the ancient fortifications rising above the palace of the Assyrian King Sargon.

Around 1000 BC, Dilmun fell into decline because of the development of other trade routes. It was also a period when Bahrain was ruled by foreigners. By about 600 BC, Bahrain had been absorbed into the Babylonian Empire where it once again flourished under the powerful rule of Ashurbanipal, an Assyrian from Mesopotamia whose empire extended from North Africa to the Arabian Gulf.

Around 540 BC, the Persians displaced the Babylonians as rulers of Bahrain. They were in turn displaced by the Greeks in 323 BC when two of Alexander the Great's ships arrived in Bahrain, forging new trade routes to Europe. With the death of Alexander the Great, Bahrain came under Arab influence.

Visitors have been coming for 5,000 years and the legacy of the ancients has become a powerful draw.

The first Arab settlement of Bahrain was around 300 BC. One of the idols the Rabyah tribe worshiped was Oraal, whom they named Bahrain after. The Rabyahs were attacked by a tribe lead by Abu-l-Bahul. When he defeated the Rabyahs, he became the Prince of Bahrain.

Around 250 BC, the Persians again conquered Bahrain, absorbing it into the Parthian Empire, stretching from present-day Syria to present-day Oman. The Parthians built a number of garrisons as far south as where Oman is now to protect their trade routes and ensure military superiority.

The Sassanians, who were another Persian Dynasty, conquered Bahrain around AD 400. They were able to establish agricultural colonies in Bahrain and in the region. They negotiated with the nomadic tribes to act as border guards to protect their colonies from the Romans.

From the 9th–11th century, Bahrain was part of the Umayyad and later the Abbasid empires. Under the rule of the Abbasids, the Shiite branch of Islam became the dominant religious denomination in Bahrain.

Later in the 15th century, the Portuguese began exploring the region. With the arrival of Vasco de Gama and his Portuguese ships in the Arabian Gulf, the overland trade routes disintegrated. The opening of the Suez Canal much later further threatened trade routes.

By the beginning of the 16th century, the Portuguese navy had occupied the island of Hormuz off the Persian coast. Hormuz attracted wealthy merchants in buying and selling silks, precious stones, cloths, silver, gold, wines and spirits. The finest pearls in the world were imported from Bahrain along with their famous white donkeys.

The Bahrain Fort, also known as the Portuguese Fort. Parts of the fort date back to 2800 BC.

By 1523, the Portuguese had colonised Bahrain, taking control of the spice trade between India and Europe previously handled by the Arabs. The Portuguese remained in power until 1602, when a coalition of forces comprising Bahrainis and Persians, under the command of Shah Abbas The Great, evicted the Portuguese from Bahrain. Shah Abbas then negotiated a defence treaty putting Bahrain under the protection of the Persians again.

In 1611, the British through their East India Company established links with a number of Arabian Gulf sheikhdoms to secure their trade routes between Britain and their Indian Empire.

After that, periods of piracy and local wars erupted once again and the last successful invasion of Bahrain was an attack by the ancestors of the current king.

It took some years for the Khalifas to gain total control of Bahrain as they were subjected to attacks by other Arab tribes in the region. When Sheikh Ahmed Khalifa finally conquered Bahrain, he became known as Ahmed Al Fatih (Ahmed the conqueror). He died in 1795 and was succeeded by his son, Sheikh Salman.

In 1820, the Persians once again rattled their sabres, challenging the Khalifas' rule of Bahrain but did not mount an attack because of the General Treaty of Peace. This was a defence pact made with the British East India Company to specifically protect Bahrain from any Persian aggression. Generally, Britain agreed to come to Bahrain's aid if the latter were threatened by a foreign power. The subsequent accession of Sheikh Isa Bin Ali Al Khalifa in 1869 marked the beginning of a period of stability and prosperity which was to last over half a century.

Sheikh Isa was the country's longest reigning amir, ruling Bahrain for 54 years. From 1869–1914, Sheikh Isa entered into further agreements with the British, consenting not to negotiate with the government of any other country or engage in any commercial venture with overseas companies without Britain's approval.

His successor, Sheikh Hamad bin Isa al Khalifa, is generally regarded as the first ruler to steer Bahrain on a course of modernisation. During his rule in 1932, oil was found in Bahrain, making it one of the first oil producing regions in the Middle East.

Sheikh Hamad died in 1942 and his son Sheikh Salman became the new amir. Bahrain's most significant economic development occurred over his 19-year rule. The standard of living also substantially improved. During one of the author's childhood in Bahrain, most of the low-income workers lived with their large families in huts made from palm branches known as *barastis*. The huts were without electricity and its occupants drew their water from a well. Sheikh Salman built a number of small stone houses with electricity and running water and leased them out to low-income families at affordable prices. Government employees were offered loans to buy land and houses but the plan backfired initially. Civil servants took up the offer but did not live in their modern houses, calculating that there was more money to be made by renting them out to foreigners.

Sheikh Salman bin Hamad al Khalifa died in 1961 and was succeeded by his son Sheikh Isa bin Salman al Khalifa. Iran's threat to Bahrain's sovereignty became more aggressive. In 1968, Iran again made territorial claims on Bahrain but stopped short of any physical action because of the British military presence.

RECENT HISTORY

In August 1971, Britain withdrew its troops and Bahrain became the first country in the lower Arabian Gulf to change from being quasi-independent to truly independent. Prior to 1971, Bahrain had a treaty with Britain who was responsible for managing the Sheikhdom's external relations. A month later, Qatar became independent. In December 1971, the UAE was formed through the federation of the sheikhdoms of Abu Dhabi, Ajman, Dubai, Fujairah, Sharjah and Umm al Qaiwain. Later, Ras Al Khaimah joined the federation. In the same year, Bahrain was admitted to the United Nations as its 128th member.

Bahrain was the first country in the region to explore the possibility of a Western style of democracy. In 1972, a constituent assembly was elected whose charter was to draft the constitution. Their constitution model provided for separate executive and judicial branches of government and a parliament known as the National Assembly with 30 members.

The National Assembly was dissolved in 1975 because the amir, Sheikh Isa bin Salman al Khalifa believed that the radical members of this assembly were making it impossible for the Executive Government to function. The National Assembly was replaced by a consultative council for the remainder of Sheikh Isa bin Salman al Khalifa's life.

Bahrain has been the continual target for subversion from Iran. There have been a number of attempted coups to topple the ruler and his government. In 1979, Iran once again became aggressive, making territorial claims on Bahrain and covertly assisting in attempted coups to topple the ruler and his government.

The most serious threat was in 1981, when plots by Khomeini followers in Iran planned to destabilise the governments of Bahrain and Saudi Arabia. This led to the arrest of 73 people. That year, Bahrain became a founding member of a regional economic political and strategic bloc known as the Arabian Gulf Cooperation Council (AGCC). Other members of the AGCC included Kuwait, Oman, Qatar, Saudi Arabia and the UAE.

The AGCC disapproved of Iraq's invasion of Kuwait in 1990 and Bahrain became a strategic staging point for coalition troops during the first Gulf War. Shortly after in 1991, Bahrain became a target for missiles from Saddam Hussein's Iraq.

The 30-member Consultative Council, whose members were mainly businessmen, met for the first time in 1993. A year later, the government liberalised foreign investment regulations and introduced incentives to encourage the private sector. Political unrest came to a head in 1994 when demonstrations in the streets of the capital city (Manama) had to be dispersed by tear gas. These demonstrations reflected civil unrest because of the high levels of unemployment amongst Bahraini graduates and the Shi'as who felt that they had been discriminated against.

Political unrest continued into 1995 as the divide between the Shi'as and the Sunnis grew, as a result of encouragement by the clerics in Iran. At one point, the situation became so serious that the Bahrain Government had to ask the Saudi Government for assistance. The Saudis sent a security force of 4,000 men to assist the Bahrain police to crack down on the rioters.

The situation further deteriorated when bombs exploded in Manama in 1996 as a result of the Government rejecting all demands for reform. The Government again had to call for external assistance from Saudi Arabia, other Arabian Gulf Cooperation countries and the US to restore order. In 1997, the amir created the National Guard and appointed his son, the current king, as commander. The National Guard's mission was to provide back-up for the regular Bahrain Defence Force and eradicate violence in the poorer Shi'a Muslim districts. There were mosque closures and the State Security court jailed 37 members of Hizbullah-Bahrain for plotting to overthrow the amir.

In 1997, Bahrain established diplomatic relations with Qatar. This was a surprise move because Bahrain and Qatar both claimed sovereignty over the the Hawar Islands.

Further violence broke out in 1998. Shi'a Muslims, frustrated and inflamed by the death in custody of Noor L Noor and the torture of other political prisoners, torched commercial properties. The long-serving hardline head of Bahrain's Security Intelligence Service was retired after the incident, signalling a more moderate stance to those opposing the regime. The Red Cross estimated that Bahrain's prisons held 1,400 political prisoners and since the disturbances first occurred in 1994, around 50 people have been killed in politically motivated violence.

In 1999, Sheikh Isa bin Salman al Khalifa died of a heart attack at the relatively young age of 65. His eldest son, Crown Prince Sheikh Hamad bin Isa al-Khalifa, who was at the time, commander of the Bahrain Defence Force, succeeded him. Some of the first acts of the new ruler included pardoning the 200 or so anti-government detainees, giving the media more freedom, inviting political refugees to come home, and ending the 25-year state of emergency. These acts almost gave King Hamad hero status.

In 2002, there was a reduction in political unrest and elections were held. There was a low voter turnout as the opposition, who were mainly Shi'as, boycotted the elections, resulting in a Sunni dominated parliament. Unemployment had become the biggest social issue and graduates regularly staged demonstrations to demand work. To improve relations between the disgruntled Shi'a majority and the powerful Sunni minority headed by the Royal Family, King Hamad al Kalifa promised that 75 per cent of the seats in the National Assembly would be elected in 2006. However, he was pressured by the Royal Family and reneged on this promise, reverting to the status quo of having the upper house of the National Assembly appointed by the King. In addition, electoral rules were changed to further dilute the Shi'a vote and the security forces harassed the principal Shi'a opposition party Al Wifaq, causing unrest.

In 2003, there was further unrest following a concert at a school which was attended by very important guests, including a foreign ambassador. On the day of the concert, there were further disturbances in Israel and Palestine resulting in the deaths of Palestinians and Israelis. The headmaster of the school called for a few moments of silence to remember the fallen Palestinians after the concert. Lacking in diplomacy, the foreign ambassador got to his feet and asked that there be a few moments of silence for the dead Israelis. The word got out about this insensitive remark by the foreign ambassador and the next day, there were disturbances on the streets, targeted at brands belonging to the ambassador's country.

In 2004, there was a petition from a wide range of critics calling for a real democracy in Bahrain. The government responded by jailing 19 of the petitioners. In a deft move, King Hamad pardoned the petitioners and called for a dialogue with the opposition. There were further demonstrations against the US and in response, the police arrested some Shi'a clerics and in the process dispensed some rough justice. In a popular move, King Hamad sacked his own uncle who had been the long serving minister since 1974.

THE WORLD'S NEWEST KINGDOM

In 2002, the ruler of Bahrain changed his title from amir to King and the country changed from being a state to becoming a kingdom. Bahrain is the only country in the Arabian Gulf to have a primogeniture form of succession as the 'next-in-line' to the throne. On his accession to the throne, the King, in a calculated decision to gain immediate support from his subjects, decreed a waiver of half the debt owed by Bahrainis to the government on housing loans. Bahrain is, in theory, a constitutional monarchy but the King wields significant power. Some Bahrain watchers say the hype about

The Coat of Arms of the Kingdom of Bahrain.

re-establishing a parliament is all window dressing. After all, the King has all the power since he appoints members of the upper house of the parliament and the cabinet which are mainly comprised of family members. In 2003, members of the cabinet who were part of the Royal Family included the Prime Minister, Minister for Amiri Court Affairs, Minister for Defence, Minister for Electricity and Water, Minister for Foreign Affairs, Minister for Housing, Minister for the Interior, Minister for Justice and Islamic affairs, Minister for Oil and the Minister for Transportation and Communications. On a per capita basis, Bahrain probably has a Royal Family the size of Saudi Arabia or Qatar.

On his accession to the throne, the Western press described King Hamad as youngish, dynamic and forward thinking. Many senior civil servants in the government and officers in the Bahrain Defence Force are members of the extended Khalifa Royal Family.

There are numerous outdoor posters and billboards depicting King Hamad as an admiral of the fleet (Bahrain has approximately six patrol boats and one frigate) and other billboards and posters show him in national dress, mounted on a horse greeting his people. Nearly every office has a picture of the king in their foyer or elsewhere in the building.

The Royal Family

Members of the Royal Family are featured in the newspapers nearly every day in their role as patrons of the arts, sports and other organisations. The wife of the king, her Highness Sheikha Sabika bint Ibrahim al Khalifa, is chairwoman of the Supreme Council for Women. Sheikha Hayat bint Abdulaziz Al Khalifa is President of the Bahrain Table Tennis Association. The Crown Prince, Sheikh Salman bin Hamad Al Khalifa, is the Chairman of the Supreme Council for Youth. Sheikh Ahmed bin Muhammed Al Khalifa, a member of the Royal Family, is President of the Bahrain Tennis Federation (BTF). The General President for the General Organisation of Youth and Sport (GOYS) is Sheikh Fawaz bin Muhammad Al Khalifa.

Despite significant nepotism, Bahrain has probably gone further down the path of democracy than any other Arabian Gulf country. The king does not allow political parties but there are voting blocks such as Al Mustaqbal (Future Block). Bahrain is still feeling its way when it comes to the role of members of parliament. In 2004, the media gave considerable coverage to the role of the First Deputy Speaker in the House of Deputies. Nearly all Bahrainis agree that democracy is a good thing but debate on what pace it should be implemented.

THE STATE OF THE STATE OF BAHRAIN

Arabs in general probably don't feel the same sense of nationalism or patriotism as the Americans, French or Australians because many of their countries have artificial borders drawn by foreign or protectorate powers. Middle

The monarchy is well-respected in Bahrain. This huge billboard of King Hamad Bin Salman al-Khalifa in Manama shows him holding an eagle.

Oil refinery at sunset—the petroleum industry is a major contributor to the country's economy.

A contrast in attire. It is common for men to be dressed in Western-style clothing (above) but women continue to wear their traditional attire when they appear in public (below).

The country's architecture is stunning as can be seen in the exquisite stained glass ceiling at a museum in Manama (above) and the splendid arches and chandelier of this mosque (below).

An aerial view of Manana at dusk.

A wooden balcony adds character to this traditional home in Bahrain.

Eastern rulers' roles and leader-image are constantly reinforced through outdoor billboards, posters, flags and the media to encourage the spirit of nationalism—Bahrain is no exception. Never a day passes without a story in the media that displays the king's readiness to help alleviate the suffering of the Iraqi people, a report on the renovation of houses or a feature that honours the Bahrain Soccer team. Everyday, there are at least three stories in the media featuring the king. The same is true for other rulers in the AGCC countries.

Democracy and the Arab World

The table below ranks Bahrain as one of the more democractic countries in comparison to other Middle Eastern countries.

Democracy and the Arab World
Score 1 = Dismal, 10 = Perfect

Country	Political Women's Freedom	Rule of Law	Religious Freedom	Press Freedom	Economic Openness	Women's Rights	Total
Morocco	4	6	6	6	7	6	35
Lebanon	4	4	6	6	7	7	34
Iraq	4	1	7	7	8	5	32
Jordan	4	6	6	3	7	6	32
Qatar	3	6	4	4	8	6	31
Bahrain	3	6	4	3	8	6	30
Kuwait	4	6	4	6	6	4	30
Palestine	4	2	5	5	7	7	30
Tunisia	1	3	9	1	7	8	29
UAE	1	6	4	3	9	6	29
Oman	2	6	4	1	7	6	26
Yemen	4	3	4	6	5	4	26
Egypt	2	4	4	3	5	6	24
Sudan	3	1	2	5	7	3	21
Syria	1	2	8	1	1	7	20
Algeria	3	2	4	3	2	4	18
Libya	1	2	4	1	2	5	15
Saudi Arabia	0	3	0	2	7	1	13

Source: *The Economist*

But not all things are rosy in Bahrain. Like the rest of the world, there are the problems of unemployment, of price and availability of oil attracting foreign investment and of regional tensions. Currently, Bahrain's King Hamad is arguably the most genuinely popular Arab leader with a stable government and a sound economy. But things can change very fast in the Middle East. Closest to home in Saudi Arabia, there had been escalating terrorism, especially against Western expats, peaking in 2003 with waves of bombing and suicide attackes. This has largely subsided but government buildings and hotels are still protected by concrete blocks and vehicles are searched. Further, events in Palestine and Israel have repercussions in Bahrain. Although not under direct external threat, there are always the Iranian hotheads anxious to ignite the feelings between the Shi'as and Sunni Muslims living in Bahrain. The Shi'as are still the under-class in Bahrain. They have the highest unemployment rate, the lowest standard of living and the worst forms of housing. Shi'a villages on the outskirts of Manama often suffer electricity cuts, leaking sewage and over-crowded schools. Some of the Shi'as are also political prisoners. Most Bahrainis, however, are less concerned about their future than the Saudis or the Kuwaitis, who despite having substantial oil wealth have ailing rulers with a less-than-clear succession plan.

INTERNATIONAL TENSIONS

Bahrain's small size and central location among countries, whose seaboards are in the Arabian Gulf or Persian Gulf, require it to play a delicate balancing act in foreign affairs amongst its larger, wealthier and more powerful neighbours. In 1971, Bahrain became a member of the United Nations and the Arab League.

In 1982, Bahrain, Kuwait, Oman, Qatar, Saudi, Arabia and the UAE came together to form the AGCC, an economic and political bloc along the lines of the European Union. In this regard, Bahrain contributes 20,000 men to the AGCC military strike force. The strength of the Bahrain Defence Force is approximately 11,000 people. The army of 8,500 soldiers has 106 battle tanks. The Bahrain navy has 1,000 sailors, crews and a fleet of twelve patrol and coastal vessels plus a frigate. The Air Force, with 1,500 airmen, serves a squadron of 24 combat aircrafts and a squadron of 26 armed helicopters.

Bahrain and Saudi Arabia

Saudi Arabia perceives itself to be the super power of the region. Bahrain and the other smaller Gulf States have always been concerned that the Saudis will push them around. The strong US military presence is something of a security blanket for Bahrain.

There have been reports that some wealthy young Saudi women go to Bahrain, considered by them to be a den of iniquity, to escape the social rigidity of their country and to try and meet some attractive Western men. The border between Bahrain and Saudi Arabia is set 8 km (5 miles) from the coast of Bahrain and 16 km (10 miles) from the coast of Saudi Arabia on the King Fahd Causeway. Each weekend, some 74,000 people use the causeway and in 2008, the number of lanes on the causeway increased from 10 to 17.

Bahrain and Iran

Iran on many occasions has made territorial claims on Bahrain and has been proactive in trying to destabilise the ruling Sunnis who are a minority. Recently, there has been a significant improvement in relations with Iran.

Bahrain and Qatar

Close to the coast of Qatar and south of Bahrain are the Hawar Islands. There are 12 small islands in the group. The largest island is 17.7 km (11 miles) long and is known as Hawar Island. *Hawar* in Arabic means 'a young camel'. Bahrain and Qatar have been in dispute over a long period of time as to ownership of the islands.

The conflict flared up again in the 1990s, when both Bahrain and Qatar announced that they were extending their territorial waters for '12 plus 12 nautical miles'. Neither side recognised the other's territorial claim. At stake were the apparently plentiful supplies of crude oil. This is of crucial importance to Bahrain as it has the least reserves of crude oil of all the AGCC countries, whereas Qatar has one of the largest gas reserves in the world.

The case came before the International Court in 1994 and both countries agreed to be bound by the outcome. When the International Court did not rule in favour of Bahrain's claim in 1996, Bahrain denied that the International Court had jurisdiction over the territorial dispute between Bahrain and Qatar over the Hawar Islands, causing tensions to flare between the two countries.

Further aggravation occurred when Bahrain announced that it was going to build a 22-km (13.7-mile) causeway from Bahrain Island to Hawar Island. Qatar upped the ante when it announced that the Hawar Islands would be included in their municipal elections. Surprisingly, despite the conflict, Bahrain opened a diplomatic mission in Qatar in 1997.

In 2007, work commenced on a US$4.8 billion land bridge linking Bahrain to Qatar, to be known as the Friendship Causeway. It is scheduled to be completed by 2011 and will include a rail link between Manama and Doha.

Bahrain and the United States

The king and the government of Bahrain remain outspokenly pro-US because they believe that an American presence will keep them safe from the Gulf super power—Saudi Arabia— and other larger countries including Iran in the region. As a reward, the US signed a free trade agreement with Bahrain.

However, many Bahrainis loathe US foreign policy. This is because some perceive US Foreign Policy to be pro-Israeli due to the lobbying of Jewish US nationals coupled with a significant US military presence that is stationed in Bahrain. Also, too much insistence on democracy could put the ruling Khalifa family under pressure.

Interestingly, Bahrain cooperates more closely with the US on defence matters than it does with other AGCC countries. Since Bahrain is home to the US Navy's Fifth Fleet and provides a base for the US Air Force, this may not be so surprising.

THE LIE OF THE LITTLE ISLANDS

Bahrain is one of the smallest countries in the world and is probably one of the smallest kingdoms along with Tonga. Being a group of islands, it has no borders with any country other than with Saudi Arabia, which is linked to Bahrain via the King Fahd Causeway. The Bahrain-Saudi Arabia border is approximately midway along the causeway.

Bahrain has no rivers or lakes. The topographies of Bahrain, Kuwait, Qatar, eastern Saudi Arabia and most of the UAE are similar, consisting of low-lying desert and salt flats where rainfall is low. This is in contrast to the eastern part of the UAE and Oman, where there are extensive mountainous areas peaking in the Jebel Akhdar range in Oman.

The Kingdom of Bahrain is located in the shallow Gulf of Salwa, approximately halfway down the Arabian Gulf (also known as the Persian Gulf by the Iranians). The Kingdom of Bahrain is an archipelago consisting of 35 low-lying islands approximately 24 km (14.9 miles) off the east coast of Saudi Arabia and approximately 28 km (17.4 miles) off the west coast of Qatar. Some 7,000 years ago, the islands were connected to mainland Arabia. Bahrain's geographical coordinates are 26° 00' N, 50° 33' E. The area of the Kingdom of Bahrain is approximately 712 sq km (442 sq miles).

The Kingdom takes its name from the largest island in the archipelago. Causeways link Bahrain Island with Muharraq Island and Sitra Island. Muharraq Island is the second largest island in the archipelago, which is

The King Fahd Causeway which links Saudi Arabia to Bahrain.

approximately 6 km (3.7 miles) long and Sitra the third largest island, approximately 5.5 km (3.4 miles) long. The King Fahd Causeway passes through Umm an Nasar Island. Bahrain Island is 578 sq km (223.2 sq miles) and accounts for 85 per cent of the kingdom's total area. The island is 48 km (29.8 miles) long and 13–25 km (8.1–15.5 miles) wide. Much of Bahrain is made up of stony desert with a central depression rimmed by shallow cliffs. The depression was eroded by the elements over a long period of time leaving a rocky area known as Jebel Dukhan which translates into English as the 'Mountain of Smoke'. It is so named because the heat and humidity of summer appear to engulf the area in a haze. Rising to approximately 135 m (442.9 ft) above sea level, it is the highest point on the island. Known locally as Jebel, the east and west coast of Bahrain can be seen from the summit although, at the time of writing, this is not possible because of occupation by the security forces. High salinity and poor soils make most of Bahrain arid. At the north end of Bahrain Island are numerous springs and artesian wells providing water for gardens, vegetable farms and groves of date palms. Bahrain has been called 'the land of a million palm trees'.

Climate

Bahrain is part of the Somali-Chalbi-Arabian climatic system. Like its neighbours, Bahrain has a harsh climate, but being surrounded by water means that temperatures are not quite as high as Saudi Arabia, but humidity is higher.

The hot and humid months are from April to October, where daytime temperatures are often 40°C or more during the day and about 30°C at night. The actual summer months of June to December are very hot and humid, reaching a peak in August when temperatures can reach up to 46°C. Occasionally, the hot summer months are modified by a cool northerly wind known as a *bara*. During the month of September, average temperature is at 36°C and humidity is 97 per cent. During the cooler months of November to March, daytime temperatures are around 24°C and may drop to 14°C at night.

The period from December to March is characterised by north and north-easterly winds known as *shamals*. In winter, the *shamals* sometimes reach gale force. *Shamals* originate in the mountains of Turkey and blow down the Arabian Gulf. During this period, there is a wind of equal strength blowing from the south-east known as the *Qaw*.

Bahrain has an annual rainfall of approximately 130 mm (5.1 inches) and most months are free of rain. When it rains, it can be surprisingly wet and floods can occur because the gutters and drains are clogged. Most precipitation is in December, where rainfall is 35 mm (1.4 inches).

THE IMPACT OF RELIGION
Islam

Islam spread to Bahrain in AD 630 when the Prophet Muhammed sent a letter to Al Munthir bin Sawa Al Tamani, the Ruler of Bahrain. The letter was hand-delivered by Al Aala bin Al Hadhrami and it called upon the people to accept Islam. Most people accepted the new Islamic religion but some Zoroastrians, Christians and Jews chose to keep their own faiths. In Bahrain, Islamic teachings permeate nearly every aspect of life.

Bahrain soon became a launching pad for the spread of Islam and developed into an important province within the growing Islamic Empire. Islam rapidly spread throughout the world through ideology, military conquest and trade. Within the first five years, the religion had made converts in Damascus in AD 635, in Jerusalem one year later and the Egyptian capital of Alexandria in AD 641. By AD 650, Islam had reached present day Afghanistan, Pakistan and Tripoli. Over the next 100 years, Islam spread to Southern Europe, Sub-Saharan Africa and South-east Asia by Arab traders.

Today, Islam is the state religion of Bahrain. It is estimated that about 85 per cent of the population of Bahrain are practising Muslims.

The Islamic Faith

The word *Islam* in Arabic loosely translates to English as 'peace and submission to God's will'. People who believe in Islam are known as Muslims. They follow the teachings of Allah (God) as revealed to the Prophet Muhammad by the Archangel Gabriel.

The exact time for prayers in Bahrain are provided by the Islamic Affairs Ministry and published in the daily newspapers. Although there are precise prayer times, there is some flexibility as to when prayers need to be said. On hearing the call to prayer, Bahraini Muslims do not have to immediately stop what they are doing and head straight for the mosque. There is approximately a three-hour flexibility at the noon prayer and for the sunset prayer. There is a flexibility of approximately 30 minutes for the other prayer times. The shops and restaurants do not shut at the appointed prayer times.

During the holy month of Ramadan in Islamic tradition, working hours are shorter. There are only two mealtimes. Before sunrise, Muslims eat a snack-type meal, the *sahoor*, in silence. After sunset when the fast is broken, there is the *iftar*, the evening meal.

At the conclusion of Ramadan, there is a festival known as Eid-al-Fitr, which literally means the 'Feast of Fast Breaking'.

You will never be too far away from a mosque in Bahrain.

It is a time to party and have lots of food and there is a lot of gift-giving. Muslims bring out the fairy lights or go on holiday for the three-day break. Some Bahrainis like to spend the Eid-al-Fitr as quality time with their relatives. Others like to go out to restaurants or visit cultural spots.

For Bahraini women, it is also a time to go to the beauty salon to have their hair and nails done. They also have a henna paste applied to the palms of their hands and the soles of their feet.

During Eid-al-Fitr, it is the custom for senior civil servants and executives to call on the King at his palace at times specified by the government. Other members of the Royal Family, the great merchant families and dignitaries also have their own receptions.

Zakat is a kind of Islamic tax requiring Muslims to give one-fourtieth of their wealth to charity, the poor or to people in need. *Zakat* includes income and assets. Muslims believe that by giving 2.5 per cent of their wealth to the needy, the remaining part will be purified. There are eight categories of needy starting with nearest relatives and then on to nearest neighbours and so on. There are some desperately poor Bahrainis but somehow there is not much talk by the more affluent about social inequality. After all, they are poor because of *inshallah,* the will of God. The Bahrain Philanthropic Society (BPS) has a quarterly support project to help the one thousand or so financially disadvantaged families. Most people in need of support are usually the elderly or illiterate.

Money is distributed from the BPS office, enabling the financially disadvantaged to be put in touch with social workers. The amount of money given to families depends on their level of poverty and their development needs.

Muslims are required to make a pilgrimage to the holy city of Mecca at least once in their lifetime if they can afford it and are physically and mentally able to undertake the journey. This is called the Hajj. It is the largest annual religious gathering in the world, attended only by Muslim men and women and takes place at a different time each year but always in the 12th month of the Islamic year. While on Hajj, pilgrims wear a simple white tunic called an *ihram*.

The highlight of the pilgrimage is visiting the *Ka'bah*, a cube-shaped building housed in the centre of the Great Mosque of Mecca. In one corner of the *Ka'bah,* there is a black stone known as *Hadschar al aswad*. The stone is a meteorite and about the size of a soccer ball. As pilgrims circle the *Ka'bah*, they point to the *Hadschar al aswad* and try to touch it. If they can get close enough, they will kiss the stone.

Muslims in Bahrain wanting to undertake the Hajj or the Umrah (a mini Hajj) have the option of making their travel arrangements through approximately 20 specialist travel agents listed in the Bahrain telephone book. They can, in addition to arranging travel packaged tours to Mecca and Medina, advise potential pilgrims on how they should discharge their Hajj obligations. There are also Islamic Societies offering a Hajj training programme for expatriate Muslims in Urdu and other languages. The lecture delivered by an Islamic scholar outlines the rites and rituals and the various steps and stages of the Hajj aided by video clips. Approximately 12,000 Bahrainis go on a pilgrimage to Mecca each year.

Additions to Their Name

Having made the pilgrimage, followers can put the suffix *hajji* for men and *hajjah* for women before their name.

The Government of Bahrain, through its Ministry of Islamic Affairs, requires contractors to be licensed by the Bahrain Government before they can take pilgrims to Mecca. This is to ensure that Bahraini pilgrims are provided with the best possible service in terms of accommodation, transport and food. During the Hajj season, officials from the Ministry of Islamic Affairs and the Ministry of Health assist Bahraini pilgrims with Islamic guidance and medical services. The Bahrain Hajj medical team of 60 members includes half a dozen doctors and nurses, pharmacists, health inspectors and support staff including drivers who are based in the Azizia district of Mecca and in Medina. The Supreme Committee specifically endorses some 50 contractors who are responsible for transporting the pilgrims from Bahrain to Mecca. To be accredited, the contractor has to appoint an Islamic scholar, a doctor and a nurse to look after the pilgrims.

Bahrainis are tolerant of other religions but steadfastly believe theirs to be the one true faith. Islam is not an evangelical religion. The Islamic world has two main denominations—Sunnis and Shi'as. The split occurred almost immediately after the death of Prophet Muhammad in the 7th century. Approximately 15 per cent of the world's Muslims belong to the Shi'a denomination.

The split still exists today. The Sunnis could be described as orthodox and the Shi'as as schismatic. There has been considerable trouble and religious tensions between the Shi'a and the Sunni denominations in Bahrain over a long period of time, and more recently in the Middle East and Pakistan.

The schism between the Sunnis and Shi'as was blamed for the slow acceptance of Islam throughout the world and later blamed for opening the way for invasion by the infidels.

Approximately 70 per cent of the Muslims in Bahrain are Shi'ites and 30 per cent are Sunnis. The Sunni minority wields disproportionate power as its members include the Royal Family, the leading Bahraini merchant families and most members of the Defence and Police forces. It is alleged that the government has issued thousands of visas to Sunnis wanting to live in Bahrain.

There have always been tensions between the Sunni and Shi'a sects in Bahrain. The tension in Bahrain between the two sects was further heightened in 1953 when a dispute arose amongst members of the Manama Municipal Council resulting in the resignation of the minority Shi'a members. In 1997, the National Guard, whose general mission was to provide support to the army, was created. Their specific task was to contain any violence by the Shi'as against the king or the government.

The Meaning of Inshallah in Bahrain

Inshallah meaning 'if it is God's will' is probably the most frequent Arabic word you will hear in Bahrain because it represents the way of Islamic life. People from the West tend to be preoccupied with time. We are always asking if we have time, telling someone that we don't have time, asking our bosses for more time, trying to be efficient in the hope of saving time and complaining to ourselves that we need more time.

In Bahrain, it is all up to God. Bahrainis are less concerned about time and other temporal matters and they put their trust in God. On the surface, this makes planning difficult. If you are at a business meeting and you ask the Bahraini executive sitting across the board table if you can meet tomorrow, his most likely answer will be '*inshallah*, if God is willing'. *Inshallah* has all kinds of repercussions. It makes the concept of work deadlines alien to Bahrainis because when the deadlines are met, it is the will of God and when they are not, it is also the will of God. This attitude can frustrate some Westerners, but losing your temper or showing your frustration won't change the will of God or make things happen faster. Most probably, it will cause even further delays. If your mindset is to anticipate delays and understand that this is the will of God, it will stand you in good stead.

Muslims believe that their fate is in the hands of God. As it happened, God was on our side when we last visited Bahrain; any appointments scheduled with Bahrainis went ahead of time. The implication of *inshallah* is that if goals are not achieved (and Bahrainis do have goals and aspirations) or if there are setbacks in a Bahraini's life, it is not their fault but the will of Allah. From a Western expatriate manager's standpoint, *inshallah* or fatalism can be easily perceived as laziness. Bahrain probably has its share of slackers, freeloaders and those that cannot be employed, but it also has its share of nationals who display initiative, business acumen and have developed substantial businesses.

Christianity

Bahrainis are tolerant of other religions including Christianity but apparently they find it difficult to understand people with no faith. So if you are an atheist or agnostic it is better not to reveal it. Bahrain is against Zionism and the existence of Israel so if you are Jewish it's better to keep it to yourself.

Christianity came to the region in the 3rd century when the area was ruled by a Persian tribe known as the Sassanians. It is believed that Christianity came from communities in the Arabian Desert, Ethiopia and Mesopotamia. Christian records in the 7th century mention bishops of the Nestorian sect, including the Bishop of Bahrain.

Approximately 7 per cent of the population are Christians. They are mainly from the sub-continent or are Westerners. The rulers of Bahrain have always been tolerant of Christianity so long as there is no interference with the religion of the Bahrainis. When the Roman Catholic and Anglican denominations requested permission to build a church, a former ruler gave them land. In appreciation of the gift, the Pope created the former ruler, Sheikh Salman, a 'Knight of the Grand Cross of the Order of Saint Silvester'. Roman Catholics make up the largest Christian denomination and worship at the Sacred Heart Church in Manama.

Receiving His Just Dues

For some reason, when the Roman Catholic Bishop arrived in Bahrain to deliver the Insigna, the 'Knight of the Grand Cross of the Order of Saint Silvester', the British objected. As Bahrain had treaties with Britain, the ruler was compelled to accept their views. After some time the British withdrew their objection and the ruler became a Papal Knight.

Interestingly, the British made the ruler a 'Knight Commander of the Order' of the Indian Empire and he received his Insigna from King Edward.

The American-Dutch Reformed Church, known locally as the American Mission, has had a presence in Bahrain since 1926. They have operated a school for many years, educating Bahrainis, which has given rise to an underground Christian movement. In some instances, Bahrainis educated at the American mission school have graduated and converted to Christianity. They have been too scared to tell their Muslim parents so they formed an underground movement and worshipped in secret. At one church service that we attended, we met a young woman whose father was Muslim and mother was Christian. She attended church secretly, too afraid to tell her father that she was a practising Christian.

The Anglican Cathedral of St Christopher is probably one of the smallest cathedrals in the Anglican world, being about the size of a Western suburban parish church. There is an Anglican Church in the oil town of Awali. The Anglican Diocese also ministers to seamen in Bahrain. Clergy at the Anglican Cathedral routinely say prayers asking the Christian God to help Muslim Hamad be a good king.

Baptists have a church in Bahrain and in addition to regular services, hold midweek prayer meetings. Some 450 Filipino maids attend the National Evangelical Church, and for Orthodox Christians, there is the St. Peter's Jacobite Syrian Church. Although there are church services on Sundays, they are not well attended because Sunday is a working day. The most heavily attended services are on Fridays as this is the holy day for Muslims and a holiday for nearly everyone.

There are also a number of Christian associations catering to the needs of various expatriate families. They include the Kerala Catholic Association and the Interdenominational Women's Fellowship.

Ironically, it was under Saddam Hussein that the Arab world's most high profile Christian, Tariq Aziz, Deputy Prime Minister of Iraq, came to prominence. Easter church services were even televised. Since the overthrow of Saddam Hussein and the violence that followed, Iraqi churches have been bombed and Christians have since adopted a low profile or left the country.

Other Religions

There was previously a Jewish community of 400 persons living in Bahrain. These people had come mainly from Iraq and to a lesser extent from what is now Iran and India. At that time, there was no friction between the Muslims and Jews in Bahrain. There was even a Jewish member of the Manama Municipal Council. They were law-abiding residents, mainly working as moneychangers or shop owners. The younger Jewish men worked as clerks and Jewish women mainly worked as hawkers, selling from home to Bahraini women. Unlike other cities, there was no Jewish quarter in Manama. When the decision was made to partition Palestine and create the state of Israel, there were anti-Jewish demonstrations by Bahraini youths and stones were thrown at one of the banks employing Jewish men. Persian boatmen and Omanis visiting or living in Bahrain looted Jewish homes. When it became possible for Jews to emigrate from Bahrain to Israel, the government announced that any Jew leaving Bahrain would not be able to return. Gradually, most of the Jewish families left Bahrain.

There are also small Buddhist, Hindu, Parsee (Zoroastrian) and Baha'i communities in Bahrain.

WHO ARE THE BAHRAINIS?

'...traditional Arab courtesy and hospitality are still the
hallmark of a friendly and peaceful Bahrain.'
—Bahrain Government Homepage,
www.bahrain.gov.bh

HOW THE BAHRAINIS MAY BE PORTRAYED

With a population of less than half a million Bahraini nationals, the world at large probably does not have an impression of Bahrainis. For those who have visited the region, Bahrainis are perceived as warm and friendly people, and are probably more worldly, multicultural and better travelled than other Arabian Gulf nationals. Bahrainis are comfortable in the company of foreigners and familiar with Western customs and etiquette. They are comfortable travelling and dining in Western-style restaurants because of their longer association with foreigners, resulting from Bahrain's history of being a trading centre.

Bahrainis probably have more of a sense of national identity compared with other countries in the region. Before 1926, there were a number of tribes living in Bahrain. They included the Naim, Bin Ali and Dawasir, all ruled by the Khalifa tribe who gave them grants of land in return for loyalty. The tribes became wealthy from the pearl trade. When the industry collapsed, the tribes became impoverished and their young men broke away from tribal dependency, because there was no social prestige. The breaking down of the tribes gave rise to a sense of national identity. This has not happened to the same extent in the other Arabian Gulf countries. For example, in the UAE, which is really a confederation of emirates dominated by Abu Dhabi and to a lesser extent Dubai, the people think of themselves as first being a citizen of their Emirate and second as an Emirati National. To encourage national identity, the UAE government has been actively encouraging its nationals to think of themselves first as Emiratis.

ETHNICITY AND ALL THAT

Bahrainis are mainly of Arab or Iranian origin. The Bahraini Arabs came mainly from mainland Arabia and the Iranians settled in during periods when Bahrain was part of the Persian Empire. As expected, Bahraini Arabs are the predominant ethnic group accounting for 63 per cent of the population. Asians make up 13 per cent, other Arabs 10 per cent and Iranians 8 per cent. The remaining 6 per cent of the population are mainly Westerners from the UK, the US, Europe, Australia and South Africa.

Bahrainis are amongst the most sophisticated in the Arabian Gulf. Having a long history in trading, they have had a longer exposure to foreigners than their Arabian Gulf neighbours.

Being a group of small islands, Bahrain has virtually no rural communities. Most of the Bahrainis reside in the capital city of Manama or in the handful of towns and villages located in the northern half of Bahrain Island. In the cooler winter months, many Bahrainis revert to their Bedouin origins by camping in the desert in the centre of Bahrain Island, in much the same way that westerners might have a holiday house in the country or at the seaside.

Most of the service workers in the Arabian Gulf are guest workers but this is not the case in Bahrain. On our most recent trip, we were picked up at the airport by the Novotel Al Dana Hotel car service. During the journey from the airport to the hotel we were embarrassed to ask our driver what country he was from, because to our surprise he replied, "I am a Bahraini."

Bahrain Society

Bahrain has been placed in first position amongst Arab countries by the United Nations Development Programme (UNDP) Human Development Report (HDP) on a number of occasions. Being placed first on the HDP reflects the substantial progress the kingdom has made as a nurturing and caring society.

In 2007, the population of Bahrain was estimated to be 750,000 but only 66 per cent were Bahraini Arabs. As with the other Gulf States, there is a significant expatriate community. The largest expat communities are those from the sub-continent and Asia, accounting for about 13 per cent of the population.

Bahrain's population is relatively young with a median age of 29 and a relatively high birth rate of 1.9 per cent per annum. Bahraini men can expect to live up to 71 years of age and Bahraini women up to 73 years of age. Bahrain is highly urbanised with virtually all people living in towns and villages; there are no rural dwellers. The major centres are the capital city of Manama with a population of 527,000 and the town of Muharraq with a population approximately 75,900. Population density is about 893 persons per sq km. Population growth in 2004 was at 1.6 per cent but this is not very meaningful because of the large number of expatriates whose numbers vary according to the availability of work.

Bahrain society comprises of some very rich people, some very poor people and a large middle class. At the

peak of the Bahrain society sits the king and the immediate Royal Family. The majority of the Royal Family work for the Government or for the Bahrain Defence Force. The more senior members of the Royal Family are either in the cabinet, or are senior civil servants or senior officers in the Bahrain Defence Force.

To the newly arrived, Bahrain with its many outdoor billboards depicting the king might give the impression of an absolute monarchy with a rubber stamp parliament together with a population seething to have a say in how the country is run.

Linked to the Royal Family is a handful of great merchant families. These are Bahraini families who have significant enterprises and diverse business interests both in Bahrain and in other Arabian Gulf countries. Before oil was found in Bahrain, they were the powerbrokers.

There are also a few great Indian merchants who have substantial enterprises in Bahrain and elsewhere in the Arabian Gulf. Amongst them are the Jashanmals, who operate a department store chain throughout the Arabian Gulf with an outlet in Bahrain.

Also high in the social order are senior executives—mainly Western expats employed with affiliates of multi-national corporations or senior executives with major Bahraini corporations.

Then there is the middle class consisting of Bahrainis who mainly work for the government and guest workers who fulfil middle management roles in the private sector.

> Bahrainis prefer to work for the government, although many more work in the private sector compared to elsewhere in the Arabian Gulf.

Further down the social scale are the technicians and tradesmen who are mainly from the sub-continent. There are Bahrainis, Asians and some Europeans working in the hospitality industry, mainly in hotels, in non-management roles.

There is an under class living in shanty districts with sub-standard housing in the north-east of Bahrain Island. They are mainly uneducated and unemployed Shi'a Muslims. Some of the boys in this under class spend their days hanging around the approaches to King Fahd Causeway that leads to Saudi Arabia, waiting to clean cars or at street corners waiting to sell strawberries and grapes to commuters.

Those at the bottom of society are the few beggars that can be seen on the streets around Bab al Bahrain in the centre of Manama.

Bahrainis are more politically advanced than elsewhere in the Arabian Gulf because Bahrain has a longer exposure to Western-style institutions. Prior to 1930, the Ruler of Bahrain appointed a British Advisor who introduced elements of British Law into the Bahrain legal system. Bahrain was the first country in the region to have parliamentary elections in 1973 and in 2001, women were probably the first in the region to have the right to vote.

LOVE, MARRIAGE AND FAMILY VALUES

In Bahrain, the family is the most important social group. Bahraini families tend to be more self-contained with a social life revolving principally around visits to the extended family and close friends. Married Bahraini couples do tend to go out more frequently in public than nationals from other Arabian Gulf Cooperation Council (AGCC) countries. They like to have lunch or dinner, especially over the weekend, at a restaurant or a coffee shop at a five-star hotel or have a meal at their club.

You won't see Bahraini teenagers out on a date at McDonalds or having a Mecca Cola at a café in a regional shopping mall. These outlets are for families or groups of teenage boys only. Teenage girls usually go out with their families. Bahraini families give the appearance of being more Western than other Gulf Arab families, having found a compromise between Islamic tradition and Western values but it has not come to the stage where Bahraini women go out on their own in public for lunch or a ladies' night. The major recreation of Bahraini girls is watching television at home.

The United Nation's Arab Human Development Report cites women's rights, education and governance as the main challenges facing the region. In most Arab countries, it is still taboo for a woman to live alone and honour killings are still sanctioned. It is estimated that in Jordan, approximately 20 women are murdered by their own relatives every year.

Most members of Bahrain's middle class have domestic help, usually a full-time maid from the sub-continent or Asia. Unlike Saudi Arabia, there is no gender segregation when Bahrainis entertain at home or when going out. Bahrainis are more socially emancipated than elsewhere in the Arabian Gulf, with the possible exception of the Emiratis living in Dubai.

However, like other Arabian Gulf countries, Bahrain is still a patriarchal society. Husbands tend to dominate the lives of their wives and daughters and male siblings have a strong influence over the activities of their mothers and sisters. The husband's responsibility also extends beyond his immediate family to any unmarried sisters and his elderly parents. The husband makes sure that any personal interests of members are subordinate to the family as a whole. Husbands tend to be more authoritarian and do not show affection to wives and family in public. In fact, the showing of affection in public can be fraught with danger. Public displays of affection are forbidden in the region, including Bahrain.

It is the husband's role to mete out any punishment if there is any misdemeanour by a family member. Punishments are usually fairly benign so long as the misdemeanour has not brought shame on the family. If a girl has illicit sex, the punishment meted by her father will be merciless. There are occasional stories in the newspaper of a husband who beat his wife.

The wife's role has historically been to please the husband, keep house and look after the children. The status of a woman used to be determined by how many children she had. Today, most unmarried Bahraini women work if they are not at school or university. There is also an increasing trend for married women to re-enter the workforce after they have had children. The number of children borne by Bahraini women has fallen by half in the last 20 years.

Bahrainis marry within their own socio-economic grouping or to someone of a higher status. At the top, sons and daughters of the ruling Khalifa family rarely marry outside the family, unlike in Saudi Arabia where marriages sealed political alliances.

In Bahrain, many marriages are amongst cousins, including first cousins. This way, the families know each other and the wealth of the extended family is preserved.

About 50 years ago, marriages were negotiated through matchmakers who were usually old women. In more affluent families, the senior male members of the families negotiated the marriage. Before the World War II, Bahraini women were married at a very early age, sometimes as young as 12 or 13. Stories used to circulate about how these girls who were married off to older men and about how they used to hide under the bed on their wedding night.

These days, the average age of marriage is steadily rising and the number of children in the family is decreasing. Nowadays, Bahrainis might receive a suggestion from their parents or relatives on whom they should marry. Women can turn down an offer of marriage even if the parents have arranged a suitable partner. There have been instances where a Bahraini father has beaten up the boyfriend of

his daughter because they had been dating without his permission. There have also been occasions whereby a Bahraini father had to call the police because his daughter had threatened violence due to the fact that he would not let his daughter date a man he did not approve of.

The Princess and the Marine

In 1999, a US marine named Jason Johnson who was stationed in Bahrain met Meriam Khalifa, a member of the Royal Family at a mall in Manama and fell in love. Meriam's family ordered her to end the relationship but Jason arranged for Meriam to travel to the US using forged travel documents and used a baseball cap to disguise her as a man. When the US Government found out about the romance, Jason was dishonourably discharged from the Marine Corps. Somehow, the couple were married in Las Vegas. He was 23 and she was 19. Apart from causing grief to her parents, the news of her marriage reached the Federal Bureau of Investigation and they told Jason that they had intercepted a man who said that he had been paid US$ 650,000 to kill Meriam. Other than causing a diplomatic incident, the event was widely reported in the media and led to the making of the movie *The Princess and the Marine*. However, the love affair ultimately failed to blossom. In 2003, Meriam left Jason, preferring the nightlife of Las Vegas with her friends to settling down...

The Bahrain Government is concerned with the growing number of Bahraini men marrying foreign women. In such an instance, the groom does not usually have to pay a dowry and wedding expenses are considerably lower. To arrest this trend, the Bahrain Government is exploring the possibility of setting up an independent fund to make grants of 1,000–2000 Bahraini dinars available to needy couples. This is to encourage marriage amongst Bahrainis and defray their wedding expenses. The plan also has the backing of the Shura Council.

Virginity of Bahraini women before marriage is still valued but it is not an issue for Bahraini men.

ATTITUDES AND TREATMENT OF BAHRAINI CHILDREN

Bahraini parents indulge their children and there is not too much discipline by the mother, especially when it is near bedtime. Mothers spoil their sons because they will be dependent on them in later life. Birthday parties are a particular indulgence. If the family can afford it, birthday parties are often held at an outside venue, at an upmarket hotel. If the children are young, the mother is usually the only parent attending. Birthday parties have a similar format to those in the West. The decorations include balloons, the children drink carbonated beverages, eat confectionery and, of course, there is the birthday cake.

Bahraini children tend to find their amusement at home and spend more time in the company of adults. Girls are taught to be subservient fairly early in life. Bahrainis do not go through the stage of being a teenager. As soon as they reach puberty, they are accepted as adults. Although Bahraini teenagers dress like Western teenagers—wearing baseball caps, brand name T-shirts and trainer shoes—they are unlikely to rebel against their family's authority.

Young Bahraini men sow their wild oats before getting married. They do not go out renting apartments with each other, but usually live at home until marriage.

NAMES AND LABELS

Bahrainis usually have at least three names. The first name is a given name often taken from the Qur'an or a paternal grandparent. The second name is the given name of the boy or girl's father. The third name is the family name. In the case of boys, the word *bin* meaning 'son of' is used to link the first name to the second name. In the case of girls, the word *bint* meaning 'daughter of' is used.

Girls are always daughters of their father and not their mother because she always belongs to her father. The word '*al*' meaning 'of the family of' is used to link the second name with third name. So if the male co-author of this book was a Bahraini, he would be named 'Harvey bin Len al Tripp' and the other co-author would be named 'Margaret bint Reginald al Tripp'.

When a young lady gets married, she retains her first and also her second name because she remains her father's daughter, but she does change her family name to her husband's.

On name cards and business cards, Bahrainis adopt a Western format. Therefore, the name or business card might say 'Harvey L Tripp' or 'Margaret R Tripp' and have the usual information of job, title, address and contact numbers.

Some Arabian Gulf nationals have another naming style, referring to themselves as the father or mother of a particular child. By using the word 'Abu' in the case of the father and 'Umm' in the case of Mother. So in the authors' case, Harvey might refer to himself as 'Abu Nicholas' meaning the father of Nicholas and Margaret might refer to herself as 'Umm Euan' meaning the mother of Euan.

Forms of Address

Arabic for 'Mr' is *essayed*, 'Mrs' is *essayida* and 'Miss' is *al-aniseh*.

In Bahrain, the title *Sheikh* is given to male members of the Royal Family and clerics. The title *Sheikha* is given to female members of the Royal Family.

Marriage Laws

It is lawful for a Muslim to have up to four wives, but the husband must treat each wife equally. In practice, most men have only one wife because treating each wife equally in every day life is quite hard to accomplish and it is expensive to keep up to four wives and four families. However, situations where a Muslim man may take more than one wife include an instance where a first wife is sick or a wife who cannot have children. The Prophet Muhammad originally declared that men could have up to four wives because there was a general shortage of men occasioned by slayings in battles.

In the West, the word *harem* refers to situations in which a man has a roomful of beautiful women at his beck and call. In Arabic, the word *harem* pronounced 'ha-ram' with the stress on the second syllable, has come to mean anything that is against Islam. But similar to the West, Bahrain has recently seen an increase in the number of divorces with more women initiating the seperation.

A Bahraini bride's hand, donned with expensive jewellery.

BAHRAINI WOMEN

In Bahrain, many women drive and have responsible, well-paid jobs. Bahraini women are economically and socially liberated but there has recently been a trend for young women to dress more conservatively. In the 1980s, many young Bahraini women wore Western dresses, whereas today, many young Bahraini women are opting to wear the traditional *abaya* and cover their heads with a *hijab*.

Interestingly, older, well-educated Bahraini women on a higher socio-economic level still wear Western dresses and their contribution to national dressing is to cover their head with a *hijab*. Female newsreaders in Bahrain used to appear on camera wearing Western dresses but have now changed to appear on camera wearing the national dress.

There is an increasing trend for Arab women to wear *hijabs*. Some say the wearing of the *hijab* is a personal expression of religious devotion, while others say it is to escape the tyranny of fashion.

Applying henna is an indulgence for Bahraini women. Henna can be applied to the palms of their hands and the soles of their feet. This occurs during the *Eid* when Bahraini women visit the beauty salon and for the bride on the night before she gets married.

Henna

Henna paste is made from leaves of a desert shrub. The leaves are gathered and laid on to a tray to dry and then pounded into a fine powder that is sifted to make it superfine. The powder is then mixed with water to form a paste. Boiled lime juice, tea and other ingredients are added to the paste to give the mixture a brown or black colour. The paste is put into a cone-shaped plastic container like a cake decorator and squeezed onto the ladies' hands and feet.

The Henna artist spends hours with her client, drawing intricate designs in accordance with the wishes of her client. Designs range from flowers or butterflies for younger women, to complex geometrical shapes for those that are older.

Henna was originally used to improve health. The painting of the soles of the feet was to protect them from the hot sand. Henna was also used to prevent headaches and eyesores and to make the hair shiny.

Bahraini women are cheerful and optimistic. The rights of women have been well-recognised, for example, the Bahrain Women's Society promotes rebellion against unrealistic traditions. Women also work in a variety of jobs, go to university, drive cars, have passports, travel and do most things Western women do. The exception is that if they are single, they are usually chaperoned and don't go out by themselves in public. Some people would say that Bahrainis have one of the strongest identities in the Arabian Gulf. They have been a nation with a government and an infrastructure, and have been dealing with foreigners longer than any of the AGCC countries. Although Bahrain has a large guest work force, Bahrainis do a lot for themselves.

Women in the Workforce

Bahraini women probably work in a wider range of jobs compared to their counterparts in other Arabian Gulf countries. In addition to working in pink-collar jobs as shop assistants, personal assistants, teachers and nurses, some do have quite senior positions in the civil service and some women are even officers in the Bahrain Defence Force.

Women generally do not have high profiles in business in Bahrain or in the AGCC countries, but there are exceptions.

Bahraini women in business attend high-level conferences and programmes including the Gulf Executive Programme, a joint-venture with the University of Virginia's Darden School of Business Administration for senior Bahraini managers.

The Ladies Make Their Mark

On the authors' last visit to Bahrain, they were quite surprised to find that the driver of their limousine was a Bahraini lady. We were surprised that in such a globally male-orientated occupation, Bahrain had a female limousine driver and furthermore, she was working at night in a Middle Eastern country. Female drivers at Bahrain Limo must be paid quite well as we asked her who was looking after her children and she told us it was the maid. During our journey, she asked us where we were from, and when we said we were from Australia, she mentioned her visit to Sydney. When we arrived at the Novotel al Dana, we were in for another surprise to see that the concierge was a Bahraini lady—another occupation dominated by men.

MALE BONDING

It often comes as a surprise to Westerners to see two Bahraini men holding hands as they walk down the alleys in the *souq*. But it's not what you might be thinking. The Bahraini men are probably not homosexual because Islam is a strongly heterosexual religion.

Bahraini men show a lot of affection to each other. When they meet, they often each kiss each other on the cheeks, or on the tip of the nose or engage in nose-to-nose touching.

CHAPTER 4

SOCIALISING WITH BAHRAINIS

'Bahrain... an Arab exception. Bahrain is cutting a
different cause. Not only may its women go out
unveiled and drive cars, they may even vote...
the country's residents already have more freedom
than those of any neighbouring country. So much
so that they are noisily demanding more.'
—*The Economist*

VISITING THE HOME OF A BAHRAINI

Many Bahrainis enjoy subsidised housing. This may be in the form of housing grants, soft loans by the banks or by the waiver of debt on housing loans, for example, when the amir became king.

There are two reasons as to why an expat may be invited into the house of a Bahraini. One reason is that you have been invited to a specific function, say lunch or dinner, the other reason may be that the head of the household is holding a *majlis*.

If you have been invited to a specific function such as lunch or dinner, it is customary to bring a gift. However, it is not customary to actually hand the gift to the host when you arrive at their house. The protocol is not to let the host know you have brought a gift and leave it unobtrusively in the house, to be opened after you and the other guests have departed.

Different Strokes for Different Folks

A Bahraini from a leading merchant family tells the story of being invited to a Western expat's house for a meal. According to a Bahraini custom, the gift was left discreetly in the host's house. Some days later, the host, having found the gift, phoned the Bahraini to ask if he had left something behind.

A Bahraini family having a meal together.

One of the first acts of hospitality extended would be to offer you a drink. In many instances, this is most likely to be Arabic coffee or *gahwah*, as they call it in Arabic. The coffee is likely to be served from a brass beaker, later poured into small china cups that are without handles.

The coffee has a distinct taste because it contains cardamom and cloves. Your cup will be continually topped up until you signal that you have had enough by shaking the empty cup. It is considered polite to have two or three cups only. To have only one cup is a signal to your host that his coffee is not up to scratch and to have more than three cups signifies that you are wearing out your welcome.

Not all Bahrainis offer you coffee when you first arrive. Many Bahrainis, especially those from the higher socio-economic groups, are very Westernised yet they maintain their Bahraini culture. During the authors' most recent visit to Bahrain, we were invited to lunch by one of the great merchant families. The head of the household kindly picked us up from our hotel and drove us to his two-storey house, which is similar to houses seen in the better residential districts in Australia, Canada, the US or the UK.

Upon entering the house, we were shown into the sitting room and invited to sit on some Western-style lounge chairs rather than on the cushions on the floor. The sitting room was furnished Western-style. Slightly surprised, we were offered an alcoholic beverage upon our arrival. (In the event you are offered an alcoholic beverage in the home of a Bahraini, it is quite alright to accept if you know the Bahraini to be liberal.) You may find that should you be offered an alcoholic beverage, the range of alcoholic beverages may be limited. In the household we visited, there was a choice of beer or red wine. As it happened, one of the authors requested a beer and the other a red wine, served by a maid from the sub-continent (India, Pakistan, Bangladesh, Afghanistan, Sri Lanka). Our host joined us with a beer and our hostess consumed a non-alcoholic carbonated beverage.

During our pre-luncheon drink, their maid laid the table. After 30 minutes or so, we were invited into one of the two dining rooms to partake of the lunch. Traditional Arab meals are always shared and food is taken from a large platter. The host indicated where we should sit. This is not in accordance with Western protocol, where the head of the household would normally sit at the head of the table. One of the authors sat at the head of the table and the host and hostess sat on the right of the head of the table. The other author sat on the left of the head of the table.

On the table was a spread of food consisting of lamb, fish, rice and a number of Arabian delicacies. The hostess, instead of the maid, served us our food. We all ate using knives and forks but halfway through the meal the host asked if we would mind if he ate with his hands. For a Westerner, it is not a habit to eat with one's hands. Our host made a joke that eating with your hands is faster than with a knife and fork. Should you be required to eat with your hands, it is extremely important that you use only your right hand. It is considered exceptionally bad form to eat with your left hand. The maid was not in attendance when we ate but when she was needed, the hostess rang a bell.

The duration of the lunch was about three hours and at one stage, the hostess excused herself, took a prayer mat

Bahrainis and Westerners socialising at a children's party.

from the cupboard and went into another room to pray for about 20 minutes. The lunch concluded with fresh fruit. We then adjourned to the sitting room where we were served black Arab tea or *shaay* (pronounced as chai) in a small glass cup with a saucer.

The other reason for visiting a Bahraini's house is to attend a *majlis*. This is something akin to an 'open house' in Western countries. The frequency of having a *majlis* depends on the social status of the person and his own inclination.

The king holds a *majlis* regularly, perhaps once a week, and this is an opportunity for his subjects to petition the ruler for favours. Western men invited to the palace should wear a lounge suit unless otherwise instructed.

Visitors should first walk to His Majesty before greeting any other person. The introduction is usually effected by a slight bow and a light handshake. It is desirable that the greeting is in Arabic. The actual greeting depends on the occasion. On feast days, it is the custom to say in Arabic, 'May your feast be blessed, your Majesty'. On other occasions, the greeting in Arabic is 'As each year passes, may you be well'. Having greeted the king, it is then the custom to sit in one of the chairs at the side of the *majlis*. The sprinkling of rose water on the hands of the guests is the signal that the audience has concluded. In the case of very important persons (VIPs), the king will not call for the sprinkling of rose water until the VIP is ready to leave. In the company of the king, it is considered discourteous to cross your legs or expose the soles of your feet. After the sprinkling of rosewater, visitors should take their leave by shaking hands with the king, saying in Arabic 'may God go with you' and then depart while trying not to turn your back to the king. This can be achieved by moving off slightly to one side before turning to walk out.

Some wealthy merchant families may also have a *majlis* on a regular basis. There is some flexibility with a *majlis* in that the time and duration can be specified, as with the guest list. Some *majlis* are for family only while for others, it is open to outsiders.

GOING TO A BAHRAINI WEDDING

These days, when the daughters of well-to-do merchants marry, it is a relatively simple affair compared to the past. It often follows the Western custom of a white wedding dress, a veil, bridesmaids and printed invitations. If you are an expat male and receive an invitation to a Bahraini wedding, read the card carefully as your wife may not be invited unless specifically mentioned. Although Muslim men are allowed four wives, nowadays most young Bahraini men only have one. Unlike the past, the bride and groom have usually met prior to the wedding at school, university, work or because they are cousins.

The betrothal is a strictly family affair that is an important precursor to a Muslim wedding. It may be completed several years in advance of the wedding although these days, the timing between the two events has been contracting. On the occasion of the betrothal, the prospective bride, represented by her father or senior male relative, together with the bridegroom, receive the blessing of the *qadhi* (religious judge) and exchange gold rings.

In the past, the actual wedding could take place at extremely short notice depending on the wishes of the bridegroom. Bahraini weddings are always celebrated at night. One thing that has not changed is that only women get to see the bride before the wedding. Along with the rest of the world, Bahraini weddings are becoming lavish and expensive affairs. Traditionally for the more affluent Bahrainis, the wedding party is split into two groups. There is, usually, a function for the bride and the women as well as another one for the bridegroom and the male guests,

Prior to the wedding functions, a cleric comes to the bride's household to draw up a marriage contract, much like a pre-nuptial agreement. And prior to the wedding itself, the bride may have a henna party where the hands and the feet of the bride are painted with intricate patterns. The actual marriage ceremony is held in a mosque.

sometimes held at two different five-star hotels. Sometimes, wedding parties are mixed. There is a large guest list—maybe up to 1,000 people. The guest list includes the extended family and the relatives of the bride and groom.

It is customary for the bride to receive a dowry of cash and jewellery from the groom. The dowry and the jewellery are the properties of the bride, but often the money is used to assist in the purchase of a house or to buy items such as furniture for the home.

The wedding process may take up to three days. After the ceremony, the newly married couple can choose to live separately from their parents in an apartment or a house.

Over 50 years ago, things were different. The wedding would be celebrated over a number of days. If one from the Khalifa Royal Family was to be married, men would assemble on horseback with weapons and there would be much mock fighting. On the final night of celebrations called 'the night of entering', it would be customary for the father of the bridegroom to throw a dinner party for men only. After the dinner, the father of the bridegroom would lead the men to the house of the bride. Inside the house of the bride, women would be singing. The men would then enter the house and proceed to the bridal chamber where they would drink coffee and wish happiness to the bridegroom.

The bridal chamber itself would be decorated with silks that formed a tent blocking the windows. There would be many suspended large mirrors and coloured glass balls and the floor would be thickly covered with Persian carpets. The only furniture in the room would be a large double bed and a table. On the table would be candles, flowers and a jug of water.

In the inner courtyard of the house, women in almost transparent garments, unseen but not unheard from the men, would be singing love songs and making sensuous movements.

In the women's quarters of the house, the bride—dressed in silks and laden with gold jewellery—would be exhibited. Her hair would be elaborately plaited and intertwined with flowers. Her hands and feet would be painted in fine patterns with henna dye.

At an appropriate time, the men would take their leave of the bridal chamber and after a short interval, the women relations of the bride would escort her to the bridal chamber. After receiving a signal that the bridegroom is approaching, the women would take their leave.

The bridegroom, on entering the chamber, gives the bride a gift, usually jewellery, and then unveils her. Theoretically, this would be the moment that he sees his bride for the first time. During the night, the singing would continue and there would be much scurrying about by the women. Before the bride and groom emerge from the nuptial chamber, the women in the house would discuss amongst themselves the most intimate details of the wedding night. The bride and groom are supposed to spend three days and three nights incarcerated together, but more often than not, the bridegroom will be able to slip out for a while. On the fourth day, the couple will move to their own home.

GOING TO A BAHRAINI FUNERAL

There is no great ceremony associated with going to a Bahraini funeral and those who attend are very close friends of the dearly departed. A deceased Muslim is buried almost immediately after he or she dies.

The funeral process starts with the body being washed at home, at the mosque or at the cemetery. The body is then adorned, as it would be in life and dressed in a shroud with the head covered. Coffins are not used at Muslim funerals in Bahrain. The grave is a fairly narrow slit in the ground and the body is placed on its right side with the head facing Mecca. The narrow slit or trench is blocked with pebbles and the hole is filled with sand. Immediately before the grave is filled in, the mask covering the head is removed so that the deceased person is 'seeing' Mecca. Women of the surviving family do not wear cosmetics, oils, incense, perfume or jewellery when attending the funeral. Friends and relatives bring food for the immediate family for three days and in turn are only offered coffee as a sign of renewed friendship. There are no elaborate gravestones. Men seldom visit gravesites and women never do. When an important person dies, his house may be shut up for a considerable time after his death.

Royal Funerals

In the case of an important person like King Hussein of Jordan, the funeral service may be delayed two or three days so that the dignitaries have time to attend the funeral. In the case of the late Amir of Bahrain, Sheikh Isa bin Salman al Khalifa, he declared his wish to be buried immediately after his death so few dignitaries were able to attend the funeral service.

Non-Muslims attending a funeral should stand to the side of the funeral party and not take an active role in the ceremony.

There is no mourning period for a widower but a widow is secluded for four months and ten days. If the widow looks at a man who is not part of her immediate family, she must bathe in order to purify herself. Other relatives mourn for a shorter period and no grief is shown in public. Mourners express their condolences saying *aDHDHam alaahu ajrakum* which means, 'May God greatly reward you for your loss'.

DRESS CODE FOR BAHRAINIS

Bahrainis are very conscious about the way they appear in public. They dress to blend in and not have any bad reflection on their family. The dress code for Bahrainis, like those of the region, is greatly influenced by religion and the climate. Islam requires Muslims to dress modestly and it did make sense in the past that in the harsh climate, nearly the whole body was covered. These days, climate does not play such a role in determining how they dress as most Bahrainis live and work in an air-conditioned environment.

Most, but not all, Bahrainis wear the national dress. For men, this consists of a long garment resembling a nightshirt known as a *thobe*. In summer, men wear white cotton *thobes* whereas in winter their *thobes* are made of heavier material and are often coloured blue or grey. Underneath the *thobe*, Bahraini men used to wear a *serwaal*, somewhat similar to a pair of cotton pyjama pants. Now, in summer, they wear a longish T-shirt or sarong-like garment known as a *wizar* and in winter, they wear Western trousers. For additional warmth,

some Bahraini men may wear a brand name jacket. The headdress for men consists of a crocheted cap or *ghafeyah* worn underneath a headscarf called a *gutrah*, secured usually by a two-chord, black woollen headband known as an *agaal*. In the past, the *agaal* was used to tie the camel's legs together to stop it from running away. The colour and pattern of the *gutrah* varies by region. In Bahrain, most men wear a white *gutrah* whereas in neighbouring Saudi Arabia, most men wear a red and white checked *gutrah*. In winter and on formal occasions, men wear a cloak resembling an academic gown known as a *bischt*, usually made of fine silk or wool, over the *thobe*. The colour of the *bischt* is usually black or brown and edged in gold thread.

Arabs of a Different Colour

Not all people wearing Arab dress are Bahrainis. Every weekend, there is an influx of Saudi men who frequent bars in Bahrain and they can become obnoxious after consuming alcohol. Try not to fraternise with men whom you don't know. Bahraini men at bars usually do not approach people whom they do not know.

When Bahraini men began working in the oil field, they soon found that wearing a *thobe* and a *gutrah* was not very practical and could even be dangerous. They then slowly began to wear Western-style clothing, but the problem in the early days was that there was a shortage of Western clothing and soon, a vibrant second-hand trade developed.

More recently, there has been a tendency for younger Bahraini men and especially those who work in the banking sector to wear Western business suits. Even the outdoor advertising signs featuring the king show him in his naval uniform of an Admiral of the Fleet rather than in a *guttrah* and *thobe*. For women, the trend has been going the other way. Nowadays, younger women are moving back to the national dress and now nearly all Bahraini women wear at least a *hijab*.

Ladies often wear Western-style clothes covered by a loose black coat known as an *abaya* which is a loose fitting garment made of opaque material so as not to reveal the figure and attract the attention of men. *Abayas* have become a fashion item. There are specialist shops in the Manama *souq* selling high fashion *abayas*. Western couturiers have also entered the Arab fashion market and it is possible to buy an *abaya* with a famous brand name like Dior.

The national dress worn by nationals in other AGCC countries is similar to that which is worn in Bahrain. In the UAE, the long white garment resembling a nightshirt worn by men is known as a *dishdasha* whereas in Bahrain it is known as a *thobe*. Women often wear a long straight gown called a *kandura* and over that, a loose flowing black garment known as an *abaya*.

Underneath the *abaya*, women often wear the latest fashion adapted to suit local taste. There has been an increasing tendency for women to wear a scarf, known as a *hijab,* over their heads. Some older Bahraini women wear a *burka*, a veil that covers nearly all of their face.

The dress code for Bahraini women in the company of her family or extended family is more relaxed and therefore the *abaya* and *hijab* are not worn.

Abacadabra!

Many foreigners living in Bahrain have heard the story of the Bahraini woman on board a Gulf Air flight awaiting departure to London dressed in her *abaya* and *hijab*. After the aircraft has taken off and the captain has turned off the 'fasten your seat belt' sign, she leaves her seat and moves off to the toilets, never to be seen again. Some time later, a completely different woman emerges, wearing the latest Western fashion. She returns to the seat previously occupied by the Bahraini lady carrying her Gulf Air cabin bag, which is not quite closed, revealing a hint of black material. A similar story can be told of a Bahraini man dressed in *thobe* and *gutrah* who emerges in a business suit afterwards.

DRESS CODE FOR FOREIGNERS

Bahrain is fairly liberal by Gulf standards, because compared to the other AGCC countries (with the exception of Dubai), Bahrain is less restrictive when it comes to Western dress. But overall, the region is very conservative in all aspects of life including dress. Women may wear bikinis at the pool in hotels and clubs or at the beach but not anywhere else. If staying in a hotel, men and women should wear the bathrobe provided by the hotel when they leave their room and take it off only when they have arrived at the pool.

Women should not wear miniskirts, short shorts or halter-tops when they are in public. Similarly, men should not walk around just in shorts or wear tight clothing.

> For a Bahraini, wearing the national dress is akin to a Westerner wearing a lounge suit. If you happen to meet a Bahraini garbed in such an attire, chances are he is either an executive or professional man.

Business dress for men depends to some extent on the job. In summer, managers wear long trousers and an open neck business shirt. Some managers, especially bankers, wear a tie. For evening functions like attending a cocktail party or dinner at an upmarket hotel or club, a suit is worn.

When the first drilling crew arrived in Bahrain in 1931, in the days before air-conditioning, the ruler Sheikh Hamad made the unusual gesture of granting them the right to wear Bahraini national dress and presented them with an outfit of the loose flowing clothes. There has been very limited cross-cultural dressing since the arrival of expats in significant numbers, except in the case of footwear. Western expats were pretty quick to adopt sandals and Bahrainis were pretty quick to wear Western-style shoes.

YOU AND THE CULTURE OF BAHRAIN

Bahrain is a cosmopolitan society where English is widely spoken. Many Western expats come to Bahrain, work through their contract and leave knowing only a handful of words in Arabic. However, in Bahrain and throughout the Arabian Gulf, much of the traditional way of Arab life has still been preserved, being reflected in the etiquette of meetings, the manner of how one takes his or her leave and how one behaves on special occasions.

Although expats mix freely with Bahrainis in the workplace and during business entertainment, the two groups keep pretty much to themselves. Within the expat community, they are further socially segregated into their respective nationalities. Expats tend to bond more with people of their home culture, especially when they are members of clubs such as the British Club and the Indian Club.

When interaction between Bahrainis and foreigners takes place, there are a few things to keep in mind:

Acceptable Body Language

It is generally offensive to excessively point your finger, clench your fist or pound your fist on the desk. At a business meeting, you should not put your feet up on the table as showing the soles of your shoes is mildly offensive. In the event you are invited to a traditional Bahraini feast where there are no eating utensils, you should only use your right hand.

If you are an expatriate male and are meeting a Bahraini man, shake hands with him. On the other hand, if you are being introduced to a Bahraini woman, do not shake hands with her unless she first offers her hand. Give and accept objects with your right hand. Bahraini men, when greeting other Bahraini men or men from other Arabian Gulf countries that they know well, touch the tips of their noses. The number of times they touch the tip of their noses reflects how well they know each other. Bahraini women greeting other Bahraini women kiss each other on the right cheek once and then a number of times on the left cheek. Like the men, the more times they kiss, the closer the friendship.

Alcohol

Despite Bahrain being a Muslim country, alcohol and sundry is fairly freely available to all. The newspapers occasionally report the police arresting Bahrainis for being drunk and causing a disturbance. Alcohol is also fairly freely available in Oman and the UAE, but on a more restricted basis. In Bahrain, Oman and the UAE, alcohol can only be purchased off-premise from a selected number of specialist retail outlets. There are only three or four companies allowed to import, distribute and retail alcoholic beverages. To purchase alcohol off-premise in Oman and the UAE, a permit or drinking licence is required, and they are not issued to Muslims. A

Changing Times

In the 1940s, the Sheikh prohibited the consumption of alcohol for Muslims on religious grounds and back then, most Bahrainis approved of his decision. Despite the ban, there was an illegal trade in *arak*—liquor distilled from dates.

licence or permit is not required to purchase alcoholic beverages in Bahrain. Similarly, on-premise consumption of alcohol is only available at clubs and hotels in Oman and the UAE, whereas in Bahrain, some freestanding restaurants are permitted to sell alcohol. There are a few 'Jungle Bars', usually associated with cheap hotels, who sell alcohol illegally to guest workers from the sub-continent and Asia. Some 'Jungle Bars' are a front for prostitution.

Although Bahrain has the most liberal of alcoholic beverage regimes in the Arabian Gulf, there should not be any overt advertising or promotion of alcoholic beverages or displays of consumption. At Formula 1 Grand Prix motor races, it is customary for the winning drivers to stand on a podium and be given a magnum of champagne, which they shake and spurt over themselves and the fans standing close by. At the conclusion of the 2004 Grand Prix in Bahrain, the winners stood on the podium without the champagne. But at the 2006 Grand Prix, the winning drivers were again supplied with champagne which they spurted over themselves.

Taking Extra Care

Western expat guest workers generally get better treatment than guest workers from third-world countries but all expats should steer clear of certain topics and avoid certain activities. Drugs and alcohol are subjects to be avoided when speaking to Bahraini acquaintances, so are topics of religion, politics and sex.

Good topics for discussion with Bahrainis includes asking about their family, but speaking only in the most general terms about the man's wife.

Bahrainis are remarkably open about their kingdom, but should you have a negative comment that is critical of Bahrainis, it is best to keep it to yourself, or at least attribute it to a third party. 'Face' is terribly important to Bahrainis and once lost, it is hard to regain.

THE LAW IN BAHRAIN
Shari'a Law

The Bahrain legal system draws on both the English common law and on the Islamic or Shari'a law. Within the court system, there is a public prosecutor who deals mainly with criminal cases. In cases involving irregularities of public monies, the case can be submitted to the parliament or to the courts.

The word *Shari'a* translates into English as 'clear path' and according to Muslims, is the law of God. Shari'a law is based on the teachings of the Qu'ran, and the sayings and practices of Prophet Muhammad are known to Muslims as the *Hadith*. The Shari'a law covers a wide range of topics including religion, politics, society, some aspects of business, domestic affairs and a Muslim's private life.

Islamic judges are not bound by precedent and often interpret the Shari'a law differently, making it a legal minefield. Like British law, those coming before the court are presumed innocent until proven guilty, but unlike British law, there is no jury. To an outsider, the Shari'a law is often seen to be unjust, unfair and inhuman. The difficulty with Shari'a law is that it was written in the 7th century and is not equipped to deal with modern society. Some decisions by Islamic judges lead to unexpected outcomes.

According to the Shari'a law in Bahrain, a wife's assets cannot be used to pay the debts of her husband. The burden of proof requires four witnesses, and so in cases like adultery, it is very hard to get a conviction. If the judge is unable to make a decision, he (and all judges are men) might ask the defendant to swear his innocence on the Qu'ran. This seems to work. Should the defendant lie under oath, the guilty person will go to hell on his day of judgement. However, there is provision for the defendant to appeal to a higher court.

The Ministry of Justice and Islamic affairs is responsible

Palm Tree Justice

The law in Bahrain was originally administered according to 'palm tree justice'. According to Arab culture, the head of the tribe sat under a palm tree arbitrating disputes amongst members of the tribe. Defendants appearing in the criminal court used to be able to claim that Satan had deceived them into committing the crime. This, of course, is no longer a credible defence.

for administrating the law while the Directorate of courts manages the justice system. Cases involving the Shari'a law are heard in a special Shari'a Court and appeals are heard in the Supreme Shari'a Court. Both courts have a Sunni and Shi'a division.

Commercial Law

Because Bahrain's legal structure is based on precedent and theirs is a simplified administrative system, it is one of the best legal systems in the Middle East. Courts administering the civil law include the Minor Courts, the Middle Courts, the High Criminal Court and the High Civil Court plus, the Supreme Civil Appeals Court.

On The Wrong Side of the Law

Bahrain nationals and Western expats will generally get a fair hearing in the courts, should they break the law. Originally, cases involving Americans, British and citizens of Commonwealth countries were heard in an Agency Court, presided over by the British Advisor to the ruler or a British diplomat who administered British and not Bahraini law. When foreigners brought cases against Bahrainis, they were heard in a joint court with Bahraini judges as well as judges who were British nationals. All cases are now heard before Bahraini judges. The most frequently heard cases against expats now are about runaway workers.

SETTLING IN

CHAPTER 5

'Bahrain has a marvellous multinational
mix of nationalities, all living harmoniously
together in a completely unique mix of cultures.'
—Bahrain Government Homepage,
www.bahrain.gov.bh

GETTING THERE

Most people, except for Saudi nationals who may take the King Fahd Causeway, arrive by air. There are actually three airports in Bahrain and two have paved runways. You will most probably land at the Bahrain International Airport on the island of Muharraq. In 2008, there are plans to increase the size of Bahrain International Airport to accommodate up to 15 million passengers per year. There are more than 30 international airlines flying to Bahrain. The national airline of Bahrain is Gulf Air, whose shareholders until 2007 included the Emirate of Abu Dhabi and the Sultanate of Oman. Now the Bahrain government owns all the shares in Gulf Air.

In 2008, Bahrain Air commenced operations as a regional low-cost carrier. The Emirate of Abu Dhabi has also since established Etihad Airways (often referred to in the West as Eagle Airways) and the Sultanate of Oman has established Oman Air. Where Gulf Air once served the air transportation needs of all the lower Arabian Gulf countries, now each state has its own airline. Regional airlines flying into Bahrain now include Air Arabia, the Sharjah-based economy airline; Emirates, the global airline based in Dubai; Etihad Airways; Kuwait Airways; Qatar Airways and Saudi Arabian Airlines. Other carriers flying to Bahrain include Air France, British

The arrival process in Bahrain is efficient and fast. From the authors' experiences, Bahrain immigration officers are the most friendly and accommodating of all immigration officers in the Arabian Gulf.

Airways, KLM, Cathay Pacific, Malaysian Airlines and Thai Airways. Because of the large number of guest workers from the sub-continent (India, Pakistan, Afghanistan, Bangladesh), Air India, Indian Airlines and Jet Airways fly to Bahrain from a number of ports in India.

If you are travelling on a regional airline, note that they observe Muslim customs on flight. On Saudi Arabian Airlines, prayers are said before take-off. If you are travelling in daylight hours during Ramadan on a domestic flight, Saudi Arabian Airlines will give you a meal in a lunch box and ask you not to consume it until the fasting period has ended in the evening. Most regional airlines do not serve pork products and other meat served is processed by the halal method. Some airlines like Gulf Air and Emirates serve alcoholic beverages, whereas others like Kuwait Air and Saudi Arabian Airlines do not, but they do have a vast array of soft drinks. All regional airlines display a visual on the TV screens in the cabin of the aircraft depicting the location of Mecca, although the authors have never seen a Muslim passenger vacate their seat to face Mecca and pray in the aisle or elsewhere.

VISAS

No visa is required for nationals from Kuwait, Oman, Qatar, Saudi Arabia and the UAE, so long as they have travel documents. British nationals with the right of abode in the UK can stay up to one month without a visa. Nationals from most Western countries can obtain a 72-hour transit visa or a seven-day tourist visa at Bahrain International Airport, if arriving by air and have a return ticket. Visitors who are not Saudis coming overland can obtain these types of visas at the Bahrain Customs post on the King Fahd Causeway. Bahrain is experimenting with the use of Smart Cards rather than passports for travel between Bahrain, Oman, Qatar and the UAE.

An Israeli stamp in your passport will deny you entry to Bahrain. This is because Bahrain, along with most Arab countries, is part of what is known as the Arab Boycott. The aim of the

Asian women travelling alone should obtain a visa in advance. This can be arranged through the hotel where they plan to stay.

boycott is to deny companies or persons having dealings with Israel access to Bahrain or other Arab countries. For many years, Pepsi Cola was the only cola beverage available in Bahrain and many Arab countries because Coca Cola had a plant in Israel. The Arab boycott list has been relaxed and Coca Cola is now available in Bahrain. Any person overtly having dealings with Israel is denied entry into Bahrain. This will be judged based on whether there is an Israeli visa in your passport. The Israelis are aware of this and often help visitors by issuing a special visa card rather than putting a chop or stamp in their passports.

According to the Bahrain government's publications, business visas must be obtained from a Bahrain diplomatic mission and are valid for two weeks. These can be extended on arrival. Bahrain has around 30 overseas diplomatic missions and at first it might seem difficult to obtain a business visa if you are not British, American or from the sub-continent. In practice, the system is much more flexible. As the authors are Australian, it should have been technically quite difficult for them to obtain a business visa because Bahrain does not have a diplomatic mission in Australia. Nationals from countries that do not have a diplomatic mission in Bahrain often obtain tourist visas on arrival and continue to renew the tourist visa from time to time while conducting their business.

A Pleasant Surprise

Another pleasant surprise will be the immigration officers, who actually greet you and smile while they process you. On our last visit, we found that the Bahrain immigration officers were most helpful. Regulations allow an immigration officer to issue a 72-hour visa on arrival which is renewable on its expiry. On our arrival, we asked the immigration officer if he could issue a 14-day visa, and after checking with his supervisor, this was granted. We then asked if the visa could be paid for in a foreign currency, such as Australian dollars. The immigration officer was somewhat hesitant because he did not know the exchange rate. After some discussion with his superior, payment for the visa in Australian dollars was accepted. After paying 20 Australian dollars each for our two-week visa, the Bahrain immigration officer was scrupulously honest and to our pleasant surprise, handed us back one Bahraini dinar in change.

Those arriving in Bahrain to work or are dependants of an employee of a company operating in Bahrain require a resident's visa. The employee's company usually arranges this. Larger organisations often have Bahraini employees in a 'Mr Fixit' role to facilitate documentation for expat employees. For those expats who are not employed by a company, it is the responsibility of the Bahraini sponsor to arrange the resident's visa and other documentation associated with living in Bahrain. It usually takes approximately one month to obtain a resident's visa. Bahrain residents must carry a registration card at all times. Having a resident's visa qualifies you for the registration card after you have passed a medical examination conducted at a government hospital. It is very difficult to live in Bahrain without a registration card. You must show your registration card to rent a house or apartment, open a telephone account, have the gas turned on, buy a car or join a club.

In addition to tourist, business and work visas, there are a number of negotiable work visas in circulation. Many of these are held by the extended Royal Family and are sold at a premium price to a person or organisation wanting to recruit a guest worker who cannot obtain a work visa through the normal government channels.

There are a few unscrupulous Bahrainis who have circulating work visas and allow guest workers, usually Bangladeshis, on low incomes to use them for a high fee.

Visas

- Pick up some Bahrain dinars before you come to Bahrain so that you can exit the aircraft and go directly to the immigration counter so avoiding losing time at the money changer.
- If you are on business and don't have a business visa, request a 72-hour visa which can be renewed.
- If you don't have Bahrain dinars, try and purchase your 72-hour visa in the currency you have on you.

In some instances, the payment takes away everything the Bangladeshi earns in his first year of employment. When the Bangladeshi has insufficient funds to pay for the work visa in advance, the Bahraini may allow him to use the work visa on condition that he hands over half of his wages for the first year. In the worst of cases, a Bangladeshi bought his work visa before he arrived in Bahrain only to find out on his arrival that there was no work visa and he is immediately deported, having lost all his money.

The Bahrain government has a policy of not permitting guest workers to perform tasks that can be undertaken by Bahrainis. This, to some extent can be circumnavigated if the job description is of a very specialist nature and it is work that a Bahraini might not like to do. An example of this is a veterinary nurse, where the qualifications include a certificate and the job includes the cleaning out of the animal pens. A Bahraini could probably physically do the work but would not want the job because it involves demeaning tasks such as cleaning out the animal pens.

Documents

All residents must carry an identity card and this must be shown before you can gain access to any services. To obtain an identity card you must have a medical certificate and a passport with a work visa.

PREPARING WESTERN CHILDREN FOR CULTURE SHOCK

Life in Bahrain for children is not likely to be so different from the life they lived in their home country. The house or apartment is likely to be similar to the dwelling they lived in at home, except that it will be fully air-conditioned and there will be a room for the maid. They will be able to watch their favourite TV programmes, go to McDonalds and have a junior burger. They will also be able to drink Coke, Pepsi or their preferred beverage.

However, at their international school, there are students who come from various countries and they might have to study an international curriculum, such as the International Baccalaureate. Students from the US may find that they have to wear a school uniform if their parents send them to a British international school. Also, they might not be able to play baseball in school like they used to back in their country, as British schools are more oriented towards sports like rugby, soccer and cricket. The French international school is most unlikely to have cricket or baseball as a sporting activity. The end of the school year is in July.

Children who wish to swim will have to go to the swimming pool in their housing compound, apartment block or at their country or hotel club. Pools in Bahrain are usually public or shared, unlike in some countries where families have pools in their own home.

For most Western children, having full time domestic help from the sub-continent or an Asian maid will be a new

Entertainment for Children

- The *Bahrain Tribune* welcomes children's contribution, in the form of drawings, paintings, short stories, short essays, poems, jokes, brain teasers and tongue twisters. Once a week, a full page in the newspaper is dedicated to these contributions.
- McDonalds Restaurant and the four- and five-star hotels cater for children's birthday parties.
- Children can join the 'Mummy and Baby Ballet', which is a ballet and modern jazz class.
- The British Club has a 'Tots and Toddlers' club for members.
- Children's videos and DVDs can be rented from video shops.
- The Dilmun Club offers junior tennis coaching and junior football matches while the Bahrain Rugby Football Club has a junior squad.
- The Al Areen Wildlife Park is a popular leisure spot for children.

experience. There won't be so much nagging to pick up their clothes or tidy their room, because the maid will do it. The babysitting maid will be a likely new experience for a young child.

Teenagers are likely to have more restrictions placed on them by their parents who are security conscious. Teenagers can't go wandering around Manama at night trying to date Bahrainis. Parents prefer their children to use private transport, and most social activities will probably revolve more around the school or the club.

HELP FOR EXPATS

There are a number of groups providing help for expats. They include a helpline, a volunteer group providing a 24-hour telephone service to listen and help residents in times of need. For people who face alcoholic problems, they may approach the Alcoholics Anonymous branch in Bahrain.

Polo

For Philippine nationals who may be involved in labour disputes, help is available through the Philippine Labour Office (Polo), who has an official attached to the Philippine Embassy. Polo assists Filipino workers by representing them before local agencies in labour related cases. While the case is pending, Polo often provides the worker with temporary shelter. Polo does not provide assistance in criminal proceedings.

The consular section in embassies and diplomatic missions are also a good source of obtaining help. For expats whose country does not have a diplomatic mission in Bahrain, they sometimes appoint a resident as a warden to offer help. Other countries that do not have a diplomatic mission in Bahrain often appoint another diplomatic mission to provide consular help for their nationals.

SURVIVING THE CLIMATE

Air-conditioning has radically changed life in Bahrain. Nearly all houses, hotels, shops, offices and cars are air-conditioned and sometimes the atmosphere is so cold you actually have to wear a jacket in the middle of summer. In many Western countries, swimming pools are heated but in Bahrain they are cooled in summer because of the high water temperature.

Most strong winds come from the north-east and they bring with them sand from the desert. Technically, these north-easterly winds are called *shamals*, but this term is now commonly used for all sandstorms that come from whatever direction. *Shamals* can last from a few hours to a few days and it is most uncomfortable to be out when a *shamal* is blowing, as the sun is often blotted out and it is difficult to see. Some expat children protect their eyes from the *shamal* by wearing swimming goggles.

If you are not used to the weather in Bahrain, it is best to wear loose fitting clothes that will keep you cool in summer, plus a hat if you are going to spend some time outdoors. Although it is hot in Bahrain in summer, shorts should not be worn except at the beach or by the pool at your hotel or club.

Bahrainis dress well and visitors should follow their lead making sure that when they are in public, their dress code is smart casual.

Business dress depends to some extent on your job. In summer, executives usually wear long trousers and an open neck business shirt, some others, especially bankers, also put on a tie. In winter, it can be quite cool and it is often necessary to wear a jumper or jacket especially in the evening. Most business men wear a suit, sports coat or a reefer jacket. These days, safari suits are rarely seen.

WHERE TO LIVE

The first expat settlement in Bahrain was in the centre of the island at Jebel Dukham, near where the first oil well was drilled. In 1921, eight army-style Nissan huts were imported from the UK and as the settlement grew, they were augmented by the newer model Quonset huts.

During summer, the roofs of the huts were carefully covered by a thick blanket of mud (about a foot thick) as

The Golden Sands Apartment Complex, home to expats.

insulation against the hot sun. Unfortunately, the mud was not very effective, only marginally reducing the temperature inside the hut. As more oil wells were drilled, the number of employees grew and work began on Awali, the new company compound north of the oil wells. Awali became the world's first centrally air-conditioned town known to its inhabitants as 'the camp'.

Expats today who are managers or professionals have the option to live in a bungalow on a compound or in an apartment. Compound amenities usually include a swimming pool, a picnic area with a barbecue and a children's playground.

Apartment complexes usually have the same amenities as compounds, plus there may be a gymnasium and an outdoor and indoor swimming pool and a spa. In 2004, the cost of leasing a luxury two-bedroom apartment in uptown Manama was around 950 Bahraini dinars per month. Leases are usually for one year and payments are usually made monthly. It is common knowledge that the lease can be broken if you are relocated to another country.

Finding Homes, Furnishings, Appliances

- Most guest workers on managerial or professional status will have a house or apartment supplied by their employer.
- The house or flat will have the basic furnishings. Employers normally allow managerial and professional people to bring with them the equivalent of one 6-m (20-ft) container of personal things.
- Appliances generally run on the UK standard of 220 volts with three pin plugs, except in Awali where appliances run on the US standard of 110 volts with two-pin plugs.
- If your employer is not supplying you with a house, accommodation ranging from shared rooms, furnished and unfurnished apartments and luxury villas are advertised in the classified section of *Gulf Daily News* and the *Bahrain Tribune*.
- The classified section of the above-mentioned newspapers also lists organisations that have lists of properties available.
- To be able to rent a property, you will need to show your resident's visa and registration card.
- Some hotels have apartments.
- Look for apartment complexes with swimming pools and outside entertainment areas.
- There are a number of housing compounds in the Al Seef district close to shopping malls with Western-style supermarkets.
- If your company or employer does not employ a service that can help you move, the classified ads page of the *Gulf Daily News* list companies who will pack your personal effects and ship them home for you.

To minimise risk, many Western expats avoid compounds or flats where there is a concentration of US nationals. In fact, many landlords will not allow an occupancy rate on the compound or in the apartment complex of more than 50 per cent US nationals.

A popular residential area for expats who are professionals or managers is the district of Budaiya, on the western outskirts of Manama, where there are a number of housing compounds close to two shopping malls. Younger expats are attracted to Budaiya because of its proximity to the rugby club. Unlike most of the Gulf States where it is not possible for foreigners or overseas corporations to own land, foreigners can purchase land and buildings in selected areas of Bahrain.

A new smart city is being built on Amwaj Island, featuring a state-of-the-art business and private communication service. Cisco Systems and Oracle developed the initial infrastructure. The complex offers round-the-clock security and its amenities include swimming pools, gyms, marinas and restaurants. In addition to luxury apartments and town houses, there is a residential twin-tower development and Amwaj Plaza is the tallest shopping mall in Bahrain. US pop star Michael Jackson recently paid US$1.5 million to buy a quarter-acre block of land in Amwaj.

Another upmarket residential complex is being developed at Durrat Al Bahrain, and like the Amwaj Island complex, foreigners can purchase land and houses.

Water in Bahrain

Much of the water consumed now is desalinated from the sea. According to the Bahrain Government, tap water is clean and free from contamination, but they recommend sweet water for drinking. In practice, most residents buy bottled water for personal consumption, including the making of tea or coffee and when cooking, except in the oil company town of Awali, where kitchens in houses are fitted with a hot water, cold water, and sweet water tap. Bottled sweet water is widely sold in shops and can be delivered to homes in larger containers.

PETS

Pet ownership, compared to other countries, is fairly low in Bahrain. You can bring your pet to Bahrain, providing that it has a health certificate but it must be quarantined for a period of time. The standard of care during the quarantine period is not the same as standards in Western countries. A few popular pets are dogs, cats and birds. Dogs are allowed out of the house but they are rarely seen being walked in urban areas.

BSPCA

There is a Bahrain Society for the Prevention of Cruelty to Animals (BSPCA) which is constantly on the lookout for volunteers to walk dogs and adopt or foster any of their animals.

There are no pet hospitals or hotels and sick animals are usually cared for at surgeries of the handful of veterinary surgeons who are mainly expats and offer services of high professional standards.

Favourites of the Royals

The Silugi Hound, a dog breed, is very popular with the ruling family. Silugis are similar to Greyhounds. They can travel at great speeds and hunt hares by sight rather than by scent.

The Arabian horse is also popular with the ruling family. It was bred by the Bedu on the Arabian Peninsula who considered the horse a gift from God, created from mist and dust. The Bedouin revered the Arabian horse so much that the headman knew all the details of each one as well as its family history. The Arabian horse has always been noted for its endurance. Endurance racing is a feature of horse racing in Bahrain, Qatar and the UAE.

ENGAGING DOMESTIC STAFF

Most expat managers and middle class Bahraini families have guest workers as domestic help and most have a full-time maid. Some newly-arrived Western expat families are reluctant to recruit a live-in maid not because of cost but because of the feeling of encroachment into family privacy. Families who do have live-in maids believe that an important benefit is having more quality time with their children, as they are free from time-consuming menial chores.

Unlike in Hong Kong where domestic help is recruited directly from the Philippines or through an agency, domestic help in Bahrain is recruited locally and principally by word of mouth. Western expats usually live in Bahrain for relatively short periods and when they depart, their domestic help stays in the house until the next family arrives. Jobs for domestic help are also advertised in the local *Gulf Daily News* and the *Bahrain Tribune*.

Western expats on bachelor status often have domestic help on a part-time basis and the hiring rate in 2004 was one Bahraini dinar per hour. Most domestics are from the sub-continent, Asia or Sudan.

MONEY AND BANKING

The original currency used in Bahrain was the Indian rupee because Bahrain was part of the British Raj. In 1971, the Bahraini dinar was introduced as the currency. The Bahraini dinar is divided into 1,000 fils and linked to the US dollar at an exchange rate of one US dollar equalling to 0.38 of a Bahraini dinar. Bank notes are available in denominations of 500 fils

(brown), one Bahraini dinar (red), five Bahraini dinars (blue), ten Bahraini dinars (green) and 20 Bahraini dinars (peach). Coins are available in units of 10, 25, 50 and 100 fils.

Foreign currency can be changed easily at the commercial banks or at the moneychangers in the *souq*. When cashing travellers' cheques, banks have a minimal fee and it is best to go to the moneychangers. There are no restrictions on the import or export of currency. Bahrain has a number of automated transaction machines located at a number of places, including the regional shopping centres.

Credit cards are widely accepted in hotels, department stores and supermarkets. Smaller shops prefer cash.

What Day and Year Is It?

In Bahrain, the Islamic calendar is often used instead of the Gregorian calendar adopted by most other countries. For the Bahrainis, the Arabic week commences on Saturday and the weekend is on Thursday and Friday. The following is a list of Arabic names for the days of the week:

Sunday	*yaum al-ahad*	or day one
Monday	*yaum al-ithnain*	or day two
Tuesday	*yaum ath-thalaatha*	or day three
Wednesday	*yaum al-arba'aa*	or day four
Thursday	*yaum al-khamiis*	or day five.
Friday	*yaum al-jum'ah*	or holy day
Saturday	*yaum as-sabt*	or day seven

The Islamic calendar is different from the universal one, it started 622 years after the death of Christ. Muslims measure their years from the time Prophet Muhammad fled from Mecca to Medina—an event known as *Anno Hejira*, and abbreviated to AH. Bahrain, being a Muslim country, uses both the AH and AD system to identify the year. In public places like government offices and banks where the date is publicly shown, it is displayed in both a Western format and an Arab format. For example, the Gregorian Monday 12 January 2004 would also be displayed as the 19th day of Thu Algaadah 1424, according to the Islamic calendar.

Banking and Taxes

- Most guest workers on managerial or professional status are paid in US dollars, Pounds Sterling or Euros and have a significant part of their salary paid into their bank account at their place of recruitment.
- There is no income or company tax in Bahrain.
- To open an account with a trading bank in Bahrain, you will need to show your registration card.

TELECOMMUNICATIONS
Newspapers
Bahrain was one of the first countries in the region to have newspapers with the launch of *Bahrain News* in 1939. There are two newspapers printed in Arabic—*Akbar Alkhaleej* and *Al Ayam*, and two newspapers printed in English. *The Bahrain Tribune* is a broadsheet and *Gulf Daily News* is a tabloid.

Magazines
Most international magazines are available in Bahrain and are on sale at the magazine shops in the hotels. Magazines include *Time* and *Newsweek*, and the array of ladies' magazines like *Cleo* and *Cosmopolitan* are available.

The Ministry of Information prints *This is Bahrain,* a cultural magazine, on a regular basis.

'Free to Air' and Satellite Television
In 1996, satellite broadcasting was introduced. There is a wide range of satellite providers. They include BBC World, CNBC, World, Fox, National Geographic, Star, Granada Sky, Bloomberg and ESPN. Viewers also have the opportunity to watch Asian satellite television stations that include UTN Urdu, Asianet, Kairali and Ptv2.

Bahrain has four 'free to air' television broadcasting stations. Programme content includes local news, religious and cultural programmes, local sports and Arab serials. 'Free to air' television telecasts 24 hours per day.

Radio

In 1955, the Bahrain broadcasting station commenced operations. Prior to this, to listen to radio, you had to tune in to the US military radio station AFRD, the voice of the desert broadcasting from Dharan in Saudi Arabia. Bahrain has two AM and three FM radio stations. Bahrain 96.5 broadcasts 'talk back' (a type of radio programme where a listener can call the radio station and their views are broadcast over the radio), news and all-night music programmes. Bahrain 101 FM broadcasts news, drama, Islamic and music programmes.Domestically Radio Bahrain broadcasts in English 24 hours a day on 98.5 FM.

Business and Home Phones

The Bahrain Telephone Service was started in 1932. Bahrain has an excellent telecommunication system operated by the Bahrain Telecommunication Company (BATELCO), a publicly listed enterprise whose shareholders include the Bahrain Government, the UK-based Cable and Wireless Company, other commercial organisations, individual Bahrainis and other AGCC nationals.

The country code for Bahrain is 973, there is no area code and local telephone numbers have eight digits. Fixed line services include international direct dialling (IDD), prepaid calling cards, public payphones operated by coin, phone cards or credit cards, voicemail and fax services.

Bahrain has an excellent domestic and international telephone service with 152,000 telephone lines and 58,543 mobile phones. Most guest workers on managerial or professional status have their home telephone bill paid by the company as part of their remuneration package.

There is a tropospheric scatter to Qatar and the UAE. A microwave radio relay links Bahrain to Saudi Arabia. There are submarine cables to Qatar, Saudi Arabia and the UAE. This is supplemented by two Intelstat earth stations, one for the Atlantic Ocean and the other for the Indian Ocean.

BATELCO has special deals for students, Hajj pilgrims and to selected countries.

Emailing and Access to the Internet

Snail mail is not delivered to street addresses, only to mail boxes at post offices. The sole ISP provider of Internet services is BATELCO and there are approximately 37,500 users in Bahrain. New users can be connected almost immediately.

The Internet is having a profound impact on some Arab countries as it serves as a forum where dissident voices can air their views about their governments. Some Arab countries have hyperactive cyber-police.

Bahrain also censors some websites, especially those that oppose the government. One such website is the Bahrain Freedom Movement.

SHOPPING

Bahrain has a comprehensive range of Western- and Middle Eastern-style shops stocking internationally known brand names and local products. Up until the 1950s, there was a strong Indian influence in Bahrain. The currency was the Indian rupee and Western expats, then mainly British, referred to the *souq* by its Indian name, 'the bazaar'. One of the best known department stores is Jashanmal which has department stores throughout the Arabian Gulf including Bahrain, with annual sales in excess of US$ 100 million. There is still a strong Indian influence in retailing. Many of the tailors in Bahrain and proprietors of small shops in the Manama *souq* originally came from the sub-continent.

Western-style outlets include shopping malls and plazas, department stores, supermarkets, convenience stores and pharmacies. Newspapers publish the names and telephone numbers of pharmacies open 24 hours a day.

Shopping in Bahrain can be like shopping anywhere in the world. Popular shopping venues include Seef Mall and the Bahrain Mall in Budaiya, a district where many expats of managerial or professional status live. The Bahrain Mall houses the Giant supermarket, retailing a wide range of premium and popular products and brands. Jaward is the other supermarket popular with expats of managerial or professional status, and its prices are lower than Giant. Futon World is a department store popular with expats living in the Budaiya district.

Western-style shopping is also available at the Bahrain Duty Free Shop at Bahrain International Airport, the Al-A'li shopping complex, the Sheraton complex, the Yateem Centre, the Gosi Complex and the Lulu Centre. There is a relatively modernised shopping centre located in Riffa Town.

What you pay depends on where you shop. A haircut in a district on the outskirts of Manama will cost you the equivalent of half a US dollar, whereas a haircut in the plush Seef Mall could cost you 5 Bahraini dinar (about US$ 13).

No shopping expedition would be complete without a visit to the traditional shopping precinct—the *souq*. This is a marketplace with a profusion of colours, sounds and aromas characterised by narrow shaded alleys lined with single-storey shops. The *souq* is divided into distinct precincts, all adjoining each other with an infinite number of products being offered for sale.

Near Bab Al Bahrain, the centre of Manama, is a more modern *souq* offering white goods, electrical goods, television sets and stereos for sale. Close by is the cloth *souq* displaying a wide range of fabrics. The Indian tailors inside the shops do not work from patterns but are good at copying the design of a dress or suit. The textiles available at the cloth *souq* include silk, cotton and wool.

Further up the alleys is the gold *souq*, now consolidated into one building, with a myriad of individual gold shops. More women visit the gold *souq* than men because they prefer owning gold which they can wear, to having money in a bank account. At the Manama gold *souq*, there are an infinite number of stores selling gold and jewellery styles, including Bedouin designs and contemporary European jewellery. Bahrain gold is usually 21-carat and hallmarked. There is another gold shopping complex in Bahrain that is popular with both Westerners and Bahrainis.

Be Careful What You Ask For

Be careful when you ask the tailor to make an exact copy of the garment. A friend of ours took a pair of trousers to her Indian tailor and asked him to make a second pair, exactly the same as the pair she left him. Sure enough he did, right down to the hole in the original pair!

If you hear the sound of banging and hammering, you must be near the blacksmiths' *souq*, where pots and pans are made from aluminium. Shopping is also available at quiet corners where the herb and spice *souq* is located. Sacks full of coriander, cumin and chillies are sold to make curry. Most of the stores do not have windows and open straight onto the alley. The fruit-vegetable *souq* and the meat-fish *souq* in Manama were closed in 1978 and moved to a new Central Market. Unlike Western retail outlets with fixed prices, bargaining is expected at the *souq*—a whole new shopping experience for some new arrivals.

TRADING HOURS

Government offices are open from 7:00 am–2:15 pm from Saturday to Wednesday weekly. For commercial enterprises, business hours vary, but are usually from 8:00 am–3:30 pm or 8:00 am–1:00 pm and then resumes from 3:00 pm–5:30pm. Five-day weeks are becoming more common throughout Bahrain, although some enterprises still work on all or part of the weekend (Thursdays and Fridays).

Many shops and supermarkets open from 8:30 am–12:30 pm and then re-open at 3:30 pm–7:30 pm six days a week, while being completely closed on Fridays.

Commercial banks trade from Saturday to Wednesday and open from 7:30 am–12:00 pm. Many branches open in the afternoon from 3:30 pm–:30 pm. On Thursdays, banks open from 7:30 am–11:00 am.

TRANSPORTATION
Taxis

Bahrain has an abundance of taxis. Most vehicles are smaller Japanese sedans and are somewhat aged. Many taxis have meters but a lot of drivers are reluctant to switch them on, preferring to negotiate a fixed price fare. The average taxi driver will usually try to rip you off. If you know the fare to your destination, you can bargain with the driver. A bargaining technique is to walk away from the driver and give the impression of looking for another taxi on another rank. At that point, the driver might accept your offer.

When travelling by taxi, it's a good idea to have a general idea of where your destination is and have the exact amount of money available to pay the driver because Bahraini taxi drivers do not like giving change. If there is any dispute about the fare, refer the driver to the concierge if you are travelling to a hotel, security if you are travelling to a block of offices, or the police if you are travelling to the shops.

At the premium end of the market, there is an excellent radio controlled taxi fleet with modern cars and drivers who use their meters. At the top end of the market, there is Bahrain Limo, a radio controlled fleet where the uniformed drivers use the meters and the fare is projected on the rear-view mirror. Cars from Bahrain Limo are usually the most recent models—large Mercedes Benz sedans. They have a toll-free number and advertise that if there is any delay, the trip is free.

Buses

Bahrain has a comprehensive bus network, offering services to all the towns and most of the villages. The central bus terminal in Manama is where the service to Saudi Arabia originates. Passengers are usually lower income Bahrainis or lower income guest workers. Western expats do not usually travel on buses because they have the use of a car or take taxis because they are relatively inexpensive.

Buying a Car

Most kinds of cars can be purchased in Bahrain, although Japanese and European brands are the most popular. Cars at the bottom end of the range are not imported because there is insufficient margin for the dealer. In 2004, Saab launched its new range of cars with consumer prices ranging from 10,000–18,000 Bahraini dinars for its 9-3 convertible. Used cars are also advertised in the daily newspapers.

Renting a Car

There are approximately ten companies who advertise their rental vehicles in the daily newspapers. A wide range of vehicles, including passenger sedans and pick-ups are available. Late model American, European and Japanese cars which brand names include Chevrolet, Ford, Lexus Korando, Volkswagon Beetle and Echo are available for hire. Most companies will bring the car to you. Cars can be rented with or without a driver, on a daily, weekly, monthly or yearly basis. Company cars can be leased. In 2004, a Camry Grande could be leased for 310 Bahraini dinars per month.

To be able to drive a rented car, you must have a valid Bahraini or international driver's licence, or a licence valid in another AGCC country. This must be obtained before arriving in Bahrain.

Driving Habits

There are no railways and the only way to travel around Bahrain is by car or bus, except if you are going to the Hawar Islands where you will travel by boat.

Bahrain has good highways and roads but you need to be careful and drive defensively as there are numerous accidents. The government is concerned about the high number of vehicle collisions, particularly on the King Fahd Causeway, and have issued brochures on road safety, urging drivers not to speed or use mobile phones when driving.

Transportation Tips

- Obtain an international driver's licence before you arrive in Bahrain.
- If you are a short-term visitor it is better to take a limousine or taxi, as Bahraini drivers can be somewhat erratic.
- Some rental car companies provide a driver along with the car.
- Bahrain does have buses but those of managerial or professional status seldom take them. Most guest workers on managerial or professional status have company cars and rarely rent cars. Otherwise, they just take limousines or taxis.

When Bahrain was a British Protectorate, motor vehicles were driven on the left-hand side of the road. But now, vehicles are driven on the right-hand side of the road, as is the custom in AGCC countries. Most Bahrainis are *inshallah* drivers who depress the accelerator pedal, putting their life in the hands of God, letting the car go where it wants. Bad driving habits include not wearing seat belts, holding their babies while they drive and allowing their children to climb over the seats while the car is in motion. Defensive driving is mandatory if you are to survive on the roads in Bahrain.

A factor contributing to poor driving is the Bahraini driver's inability to see out of the corner of his or her eye because of the headdress. The *gutrah* and *hajeb* worn by men and woman respectively has material falling down both sides of the face, obscuring peripheral vision. Thus, the Bahraini drivers can only see strictly frontwards.

Driving a car when you are drunk is illegal. Many developed nations have laws relating to the amount of alcohol drivers can have in their blood. The police enforce the law by randomly stopping drivers on the roads, requiring them to blow into a breathalyser to measure their blood-alcohol

content. In Bahrain, the police do not use breathalysers but determine whether a driver is drunk by the smell of alcohol on the breath, and whether the driver can walk straight.

Bahrain has good quality highways connecting the main towns. Petrol is very inexpensive. As with all cities, the traffic slows down during the rush hour. Like many major cities, driving on Bahrain's roads during peak periods can be a frustrating experience. Roundabouts and road junctions are the main cause of delays. There are occasional reports of road rage in the newspapers, usually committed by Bahrainis towards guest workers from the sub-continent.

Navigation Tips

Unlike in many developed countries in the world, where articulating your address is to give your number in the street and the suburb or district where you live, in Bahrain it is by reference to a prominent landmark.

Road Accidents

There are over 300,000 cars in Bahrain. Anecdotal evidence suggests that there are over 40,000 accidents per year (or one every two minutes), making Bahrain, on a per capita basis, one of the highest motor vehicle accident countries in the world. The major causes of car collisions are speeding on the roads and failure of drivers in taking care when changing lanes. While driving on the highways, Bahraini drivers often fail to look in the rearview mirror and use the car's indicator lights to ensure that the coast is clear before changing lanes. Nearly every day, the newspapers report stories about car collisions. More worrying are collisions arising from cars being hit in the back. Residents in the Adliya district where there are a number of restaurants, complain of reckless driving by motorists late at night.

In Bahrain, a vehicle cannot be removed from a collision site until the police have attended and apportioned blame. This causes traffic delays. Panel beaters will not repair a car involved in an accident until the owner presents a police document authorising the repair.

It is not uncommon to see accidents on the roads in Bahrain.

HEALTH

Modern health came first to Bahrain in 1900 with the opening of the Victoria Hospital and later the American Mission Hospital. There is a free medical service to all residents of Bahrain. Bahrain has an extensive hospital and state health centre network. Guest workers who do not have medical insurance are admitted to charity wards in the hospitals.

The Al Sulmaniah Medical Complex is one of the most advanced diagnostic and medical facilities in the region. Bahrain has four government hospitals, three private hospitals plus a military hospital. The Bahrain Defence Force Hospital (BDF) is open to civilians and has been visited by approximately 60 per cent of Bahrain's population, seeing 1,300 patients a day. The hospital offers a free service to all Bahrainis and guest workers employed by the government. It has a national chest pain clinic developed jointly with the Shaikh Mohammad bin Khalifa bin Salman Al Khalifa Cardiac Centre, a neo-natal and orthopaedics and trauma clinic.

There are also specialist hospitals focusing on renal diseases, the International Hospital of Bahrain that focuses on the management of sport injuries and the Ibn Al-Nafees Hospital for children.

There are also 19 government medical centres and five maternity centres. The government, in 1976, made provision for a wide range of medical benefits including pensions, sickness and industrial injury allowances, unemployment benefits, maternity and family allowances. In 1997, there were 100 doctors and 238 nurses per 100,000 persons. Bahrain's health service has an electronic information system, where health professionals can access the latest medical research, drug information and patient educational resources via a new Electronic Medical Library. Bahrain is looking overseas for their supply of health professionals. In 2007, there were some 200 Filipino nurses working in Bahrain.

Health and Hospitals

- For most guest workers of managerial and professional status, the remuneration package usually includes free medical treatment for employees and their families.
- All employees of the Bahrain Government including guest workers receive free medical treatment at Government Hospitals and Medical Centres.
- Short-term visitors to Bahrain who do not have employer medical programmes should take out medical insurance.
- Always drink bottled beverages and do not buy cooked food from street vendors.

EDUCATION

Education was traditionally the responsibility of the Imam, and boys would go to the mosque to study the Qu'ran.

Bahrain has led the way in education in the region. The first modern primary school was opened in 1919 and the first primary school for girls was opened in 1928. These were the very first schools in the Arabian Gulf. Until the 1970s, the UAE only had two girls' schools.

The first technical school was opened in 1936 and the first secondary school for girls was opened in 1951.

It is compulsory for children to attend school between the ages of six and sixteen. The overall literacy rate is 86.2 per cent. Male literacy is 89.8 per cent and female is 80.8 per cent. Education is free in Bahrain. Children start to learn English in primary school.

There are 218 schools in Bahrain, 180 are government-run and 38 are private institutions including kindergartens, primary, secondary and tertiary schools. There are also boarding secondary schools. Some schools, for example, St Christopher's and the British School of Bahrain, offer a British syllabus while the Bahrain American (International) School offers an American curriculum. Other international schools include the French School and the Indian School that was founded in 1950 at Isa Town. There is also a Montessori school.

A religious school that was established in 1943 to teach students the Shari'a law became known as the Religious Institute in 1960.

In the tertiary sector, a teachers college was opened in 1966 and the Khaliji Technology College was incorporated into the Bahrain University in 1968. The Gulf University commenced operations with a faculty of medicine in 1996. There are also a number of vocational institutions, including an Institute of Hotel Management, offering courses under the auspices of the University of London and Gulf University.

Bahrain has a number of private and government universities, including the Royal University for Women, with some offering courses in distance learning. The

Children who attend religious school.

University of Bahrain is the largest university, although the Gulf University was the first to have a campus in Bahrain and among the AGCC countries. Before the Gulf University, educated Bahraini parents allowed their talented sons and daughters to attend the prestigious American University in Beirut to obtain Bachelor and higher degrees.

Recently, New Zealand has become a popular destination for Bahrainis wanting to obtain overseas degrees, especially among students with King Abdullah scholarships. Although Bahrain has been a leader in the education sector in the Arabian Gulf, it is falling behind in the private tertiary sector—Qatar has campuses of five pretigious US universities, the UAE has INSEAD, a well-known Paris-based business school, while Sorbonne University has set up a campus in Abu Dhabi.

SECURITY IN BAHRAIN

Although Bahrain has a low crime rate, there is a rascal element in the community. There are newspaper reports from time to time of young uneducated men who have sexually attacked Asian maids. In 2004, the *Gulf Daily News* ran the story of an alleged rape of a recently arrived Sri Lankan housemaid by her Bahraini employer. After the story appeared in the newspaper, she was summoned to the Justice Department accompanied by a representative from the Bahrain Centre for Human Rights whose Migrant Worker Group took up the case. They told the Justice Department that they knew of at least ten cases of alleged abuse by employers. According to newspaper reports, the Public Prosecutor is often reluctant to lay charges against Bahrainis who deny the allegations.

Although Bahrain is very safe, Bahraini louts sometimes attack sub-continental men and snatch their mobile phones or wallets. It's a good idea to lock your car and take your wallet and mobile phone with you when you leaved your parked car in Bahrain. The newspapers report stories of cash and mobile phones being stolen from cars, mainly by young people.

Some Petty Criminals Have a Conscience
The *Gulf Daily News* reported a story about a thief who stole a car and then phoned the owner's wife, telling her where he had left the car. He was able to contact the owner's wife because she had left her mobile phone in the car.

Terrorism is a major threat to security in Bahrain. There is a group calling itself Al Qaeda in the Arabian Peninsula which has been active in Saudi Arabia, kidnapping, shooting and beheading Americans working in the kingdom. Of concern is the violence that goes beyond the supposed enemies of Islam, meaning Westerners, but also the ruling Al Saud family who is seen to be aligned with them. On the positive side, security forces have arrested top lieutenants of *Jihad* cells operating in Bahrain and Morocco. A handful of Bahraini nationals have also been held at the US military detention centre at Guantanamo Bay in Cuba.

FOOD AND ENTERTAINING

CHAPTER 6

'If there is not more than enough (food),
there is not enough.'
—Arab saying

TYPES OF CUISINE

With an international guest workforce from the Americas, Asia, Australasia and Europe, there is an abundance of cuisines available in food outlets. Hotels, restaurants and clubs offer a wide selection of food, ranging from fine dining at five-star hotels to burgers and pizzas at fast food outlets. Bahrain has a full range of international brand name products and fast food outlets. There are even some homegrown fast food outlets such as the pizza chain, Caesar's, and the hamburger chain, Jasmi's, with a livery remarkably similar to McDonalds. In the beverage area, Bahrainis are persuaded to be loyal to their home culture by drinking Mecca Cola rather than Coke or Pepsi.

There re specialist restaurants of almost every type in Bahrain, some offering entertainment from a live band playing Western music and others having musicians playing Arab music, providing a lively atmosphere particularly over the weekend. For those looking for European-style food, there is a choice of international, Mediterranean, French and Italian restaurants. Asian food is also available; offerings include Chinese, Japanese, Indian, Filipino and Thai restaurants. There are authentic Indian and Pakistani restaurants, some exclusively vegetarian. Plus, there are Eurasian and Tex-Mex outlets.

Bahrainis leverage on Pepsi Cola and Coca Cola brands, creating their own Mecca Cola.

LOCAL DISHES AND INGREDIENTS

Dates, fish and rice play a major role in the diet of a Bahraini. At a traditional Bahraini banquet—usually held outdoors but not seen much these days—there are no tables or chairs and guests sit on the floor. Prior to the meal, they rinse their hands in water poured by a servant from a copper ewer.

The servants then carry the food in, on large copper trays containing mounds of rice and a whole roasted sheep or chicken, hard boiled eggs, stewed meat, currants and plenty of dates. The trays are placed on mats and there are cushions for the diners to lean on.

There is not much conversation during the meal as this is an occasion for eating and not talking. If it is an all-Arab affair, there are no utensils but if there are foreign visitors, the host may provide knives and forks. Guests help themselves from the large copper trays, conveying the food to the mouth by squeezing it into little balls using the right hand only. It is a serious breach of etiquette to use the left hand. Foreigners often find it difficult to squeeze the food into little balls. At the banquet, the host may personally offer some delicacy to his principal guest by detaching the tongue or brain of a sheep and handing it to him. The guest should not decline the offer by the host, but he or she is not required to eat it. During the conclusion of the meal, hands are washed again and toothpicks are issued.

If a Bahraini has invited you for dinner, the meal will more likely be served indoors and you will sit at a table on chairs, use knives, forks and spoons, eat fresh fruit and branded ice cream.

The Bahraini cuisine is similar to other Middle Eastern countries and includes savoury pastries, *mezze*, chickpea, *hummus*, rice, lamb, chicken spiced mincemeat and Arabic bread called *khubbis*. Muslims are not allowed to consume pork because the Islamic law judges the pig to be *haram* or forbidden, as pigs are considered unclean animals. All other meat consumed by Muslims need to be killed according to Islamic law, by the halal method, where the animal's throat is cut and the blood is drained off. Beef is not featured in traditional dishes.

The best known traditional dish of Bahrain is *machbous*—fish or meat served with rice. Other popular Bahraini dishes that can be purchased at the *souq* include *muhammars*, a brown sweet rice served with sugar or dates and *sambousas*, small fried potato snacks and crispy pastry cases filled with meat or cheese or sugar. A popular sweet found in the *souq* is *halwa*, a kind of green sticky sweet filled with spices and nuts.

Typical Dishes in Bahrain

The traditional Bahraini banquet consists of roasted whole sheep served on a mountain of rice. The sheep is stuffed with whole chickens, and in the chickens are hard boiled eggs. Thin, brittle sheets of bread, bowls of stewed meat, dates and sour milk with lumps of cream floating on it and a pudding made of corn flour are also served. These days, Bahrainis usually eat almost anything that is not forbidden under the Islamic law.

Food served at a luncheon or dinner party might consist of an assortment of Lebanese appetisers known as *mezze*; *hummus* which is puréed chickpeas mixed with *tahini*, lemon juice and crushed garlic; rice, meat and chicken exotically spiced with cloves, turmeric, cardamon and saffron.

Special dishes usually served on special occasions include *harees* (made from meat and wheat seasoned with lime), which is slowly cooked over charcoal for approximately six hours and puréed to form a meat porridge.

Another special dish is *arayes* whose basic ingredient is spiced mincemeat fried inside the Arab bread known as *khubbis*.

Most Bahraini meals conclude with a serving of fresh fruit. Sometimes foreign guests are served ice cream.

EATING OUT

Bahrain has a wide range of restaurants and cafés. Hotels have a variety of restaurants. At the premium end of the market, most five-star hotels have a fine dining room, a coffee shop for more informal meals and a dining room serving ethnic food. The Carlton Rex is well known for its Indian restaurant, while the Hilton is well known for its Japanese restaurant.

Jasmi's, a homegrown hamburger chain.

At the lower end, fast food can be consumed at McDonalds and lamb on a spit can be purchased from street vendors, although buying food from the streets is not encouraged. The two- and three-star hotels like the Bristol serve good value pub grub.

In the mid-price range, there are the coffee shops at hotels and shopping malls. There is a cluster of freestanding restaurants in the Adliya district in Manama. Many hotels offer a good buffet lunch on a Friday. On certain days, some hotels offer during meals an unlimited amount of wine or champagne for the price of a glass. Pubs and bars at various hotels also have a 'happy hour', where the prices of beverages are reduced.

Business entertaining often takes place at a handful of five-star hotels or at more prestigious locations such as the British Club or the Dilmun Club. During major events like the Formula 1 Grand Prix, there are corporate marquis. Like most countries, long business lunches are a thing of the past.

BUYING FOOD

Consumers have the choice of buying food and spices from the traditional food *souq* or Western-style supermarkets and convenience stores. Nearly all expats buy their food from the two major supermarkets or the convenience stores in Manama that are stocked with imported and local products. Families living in Awali buy their food from the oil company commissary, the equivalent of a small supermarket.

Pork can be purchased in Bahrain but is labelled as white beef or steak. Fresh fruit and vegetables are expensive and can be purchased from a supermarket, the *souq* or from vendors who operate trolleys on the street. Local fruit and vegetables are grown using poor quality irrigation water and should be thoroughly washed before cooking. Grocery products are reasonably priced and meat is relatively inexpensive.

COFFEE

Serving and drinking coffee is a very important part of Arab hospitality and is a traditional part of the welcoming ceremony. It is considered most impolite to refuse the offer

of coffee and it is considered good manners to drink two or three cups. It is also not good manners to drink only one cup as this signals to your host that their coffee is not good enough. To consume more than three cups is to be wearing out your welcome.

How to Make Arabic Coffee

To make Arabic coffee, three cupfuls of water and a rounded teaspoon of Arabic coffee known as *gahwah* are poured into a saucepan and then boiled for 2 minutes. Then there is a relaxation process, allowing time for the traditional greetings and welcome.

Cardamom and saffron are then added to the rosewater and the liquid is then gently poured from the saucepan into a brass coffeepot with a long spout known as a *dalla*, making sure that the sediment remains in the saucepan. The coffee is then left to brew for 5–10 minutes and then served from the *dalla* into a small cup without a handle known as a *finjan* or *kuup*. Coffee is first served to the senior guests and then to the junior guests.

The guest should receive the *finjan* or *kuup* in the right hand. Your *finjan* or *kuup* (small cup without a handle) will continue to be refilled until you indicate that you have had enough coffee, by shaking the cup from side to side. You will very often, although not always, be offered tea or coffee when visiting a business premise or someone's home.

Arab coffee is an acquired taste, strange at first to foreigners but very much a part of life in the Arabian Gulf and other Arab countries. It is essential that visitors should become familiar with the coffee ceremony.

TRADITIONAL COFFEE SHOPS AND THE HUBBLE BUBBLE

In Bahrain, there are two types of coffee shops. The traditional coffee shops in the *souq* serve Arabic coffee or *gahwah*. Western-style coffee shops are mainly found in the shopping

Bahraini men at a traditional coffee shop.

malls or five-star hotels, serving American-style coffee, cappuccinos and café latte.

Traditional coffee shops are usually frequented by older men who often smoke rosewater filled hookah pipes that are also known as 'hubble-bubble' or *shisha*. Other Bahrainis may choose to smoke cigarettes while drinking their coffee. Unlike most Western countries, Bahrain has few regulations regarding smoking in public. In 2007, however, the government restricted the smoking of hubble bubble pipes to inside and outside traditional coffeeshops and banned the practice of smoking outside other shops in the *souq*. Even the more upmarket hotels serve *gahwah* in their lobbies and have hookah pipes available mainly for their male Saudi guests. Interestingly, at the Novotel al Dana where the authors stayed on their last visit, there were approximately 30 hookah pipes available for guests attending conferences.

In Bahrain and the Arabian Gulf, only men smoke hookah pipes, but this is not the case in Beirut or Cairo. Women smoking water pipes in these cities has become quite common and hence the spectacle of more liberated Arab women has become an attraction for Arabian Gulf Arabs.

Younger Bahrainis much prefer to have a cappuccino or a latte coffee at a Western-style coffee shop, usually located in a Western-style shopping mall. These cafés also serve teacakes, pastries, ice cream and soft drinks.

'Bahrain is right up there in the mass tourism stakes
with 2.7 million arrivals each year but 80 per cent
of them are Saudis flooding across the 25-km
King Fahd Causeway. These weekend refugees
from an austere regime blend into a population
which shares their cultural and religious
heritage—with a few crucial differences.'
—*Melbourne Herald Sun* Newspaper

THE ISLANDS

Bahrain is a land of golden smiles—that's how tourist brochures describe it. Bahrain Island is by far the largest island in the group, some 48 km (30 miles) long and 13–25 km (8–16 miles) wide, with an area of approximately 583 sq km (225 sq miles). Bahrain Island is linked to Muharraq Island via the Shaikh Isa and Shaikh Hamad causeways. The first causeway linking the islands was completed in 1942. A causeway on the Tawon Highway links Bahrain Island to Sitra Island—in 2007, some 74.2 million Bahrain dinars was spent upgrading this causeway.

The King Fahd Causeway links Bahrain to Saudi Arabia. The causeway was completed in 1986 and passes through Umm Na'san island (whose name translates into English as 'Mother of Drowsiness'), a sanctuary for wildlife.

Muharraq, the second largest island in the group is approximately 6 km (4 miles) long. The Bahrain International airport is located there. Muharraq Island was where most of the extended Royal families used to stay.

Sitra, the third largest island in the group, is approximately 5.5 km (3 miles) long, housing an industrial complex, an oil tank farm and is a port for oil tankers and aluminium bulk carriers.

The other islands of significant size are Nabih, Saleh and Jiddah East of Bahrain Island. To the south-east are 16 small islands that make up the Hawar group. The largest island is 19 km (12 miles) long and 1 km (0.6 miles) wide, has a similar shape to Bahrain and is called Hawar, or young camel, suggesting that it is an offspring from the main land mass—Bahrain Island. There is a resort hotel on Hawar Island which offers guests overnight packages, prices starting from 18 Bahraini dinars. Day trips can be made from Bahrain Island by launch (small ship or boat) for 8 Bahraini dinars.

There are numerous other islands in the archipelago, visited only by migrating birds, that are little more than outcrops of rock or have become part of the larger islands.

THE TOWNS

Manama translates into English as 'the sleeping place' and is the capital and major city located on the north of Bahrain Island. It is a cosmopolitan city with a population of approximately 150,000 people. Features of the city include high-rise bank buildings, nearly 100 hotels, an impressive esplanade counterbalanced by the older city with a colonial ambience, narrow streets and the *souq* selling exotic products including frankincense from Oman and other essences. The Al Seef district of Budaiya on the western outskirts of Manama is a popular area for more affluent expats to live in, usually on housing compounds.

Muharraq is Bahrain's second largest and oldest town with a population of approximately 76,000. It was a centre for pearl merchants and homeport for the pearling fleet. Muharraq used to be the capital of Bahrain and where the first Sheikh Isa had a palace. Muharraq also used to be the centre for *dhow* building. There are two historic houses on Muharraq island—Bait Shaikh Isa bin Ali and Bait Siyadi, which give visitors a view of what Bahrain was like before oil was found. Shaikh Isa house is one of the oldest in Muharraq and was lived in by members of the ruling Al Khalifa family in the 19th century. It was used as a guesthouse until 1973. Siyadi house is open to the public and is a good example of a pearl merchant's house. At that time, all other houses were limited to a single-storey so that they could not overlook the ruler's palace.

In those days, a great deal of activity was undertaken on the roofs of houses. Children would play on the roof,

A shop in the Manama *souq*.

parents would relax and in summer, the family would sleep on the roof.

Isa town, which is located on the eastern side of Bahrain, was specially designed as a new town and was built in 1968. In addition to houses, it has a swimming pool, sports stadium, shops, a mosque and a health centre. Isa town is also home to the University of Bahrain and the Ministry of Information. The Aysha Ahmed Almoayyed Majlis is located in Isa town and may be used by residents for weddings, lectures, condolence meetings and other functions free of charge.

Riffa is the home to one of the King's palaces and one of the best golf courses in the Middle East, and Zallaq is best known for its Grand Prix race-track and is also the area where Gulf University, the first tertiary institute in the Arabian Gulf has its campus. There are two private beaches there. One beach is for the exclusive use of the king and the other is for employees of the Bahrain Petroleum Company who live in Awali town.

Hamad Town, located on the western side of Bahrain, was also designed as a new town and built in 1984. The houses have been designed to reflect modern Arab architecture. Hamad town has all the features of a modern town, including shops, schools, parks a health centre and a museum.

THE COUNTRYSIDE

Bahrain's world-famous prehistoric cemeteries are located on six sites in the northern half of Bahrain Island. There are over 150,000 burial mounds built over a period of 500 years. Archaeologists believe that these burial mounds relate to two distinct civilisations, Dilmun and Tylos, some 2,000 years apart.

Muraqib refers to the mounds which are dome shaped, 8–24 m (26–79 ft) high and range from 5 m (16 ft) to over 30 m (98 ft) in diameter, depending on the importance of the occupant. Unlike the ancient burial mounds in Egypt and Mesopotamia, these graves were given elaborate funerals, perhaps confirming that Dilmun was a wealthy land. Dilmun was also supposed to be the land of immortals and this might explain the belief that with the elaborate graves, all people could be reborn and gain life after death. The so-called 'Royal Tombs' are located in the north-east of Bahrain Island near the town of A'ali. The Royal tombs are 12–15 m (39–49 ft) high and have a diameter of approximately 45 m (148 ft).

South of Awali town is mainly underdeveloped desert and at the very tip of the island is a small peninsula called Ras al Barr. A police permit is required to travel to the southern half of Bahrain Island.

The Adhari pool, more popularly known as the 'virgin's pool', is now part of a landscaped national park. Located between Manama and Isa town, the freshwater pool is surrounded by groves and gardens. The water for the pool is from Bahrain's largest underground spring. One of the authors used to swim regularly at the virgin's pool and even today it is a popular bathing spot. The pool is also the home to fish and tortoises.

The Al Areen Wildlife Sanctuary, opened in 1976, is a 10 sq km (4 sq mile) park located in the south-west of Bahrain Island and is dedicated to the preservation of Arabian wildlife and other endangered species. The park is divided into two parts; one open to the public and the other is an off-limits reserve where access is only possible with special permission. Access to the park is by bus from the main entrance that follows a sealed road where the animals and birds can be observed.

The sanctuary contains the Arabian oryx, sand gazelles and zebras. Wild birds found in the sanctuary include falcons, osprey, sparrows, green parakeets, barn owls and a variety of ducks. Other habitat includes geckos, poisonous and non-poisonous snakes, mongoose introduced from India, bats, frogs, terrapins, herons, egrets and bitterns. The Al Areen Wildlife Park has a strong association with the Suliman Falcon Centre. The park has become a leading conservation organisation in the Middle East.

The sea around Bahrain is very salty and in summer, it is too warm to swim in. Towards the southern tip of Bahrain Island is the Durrat Al Bahrain or the Aqua Park. There are 13 state-of-the-art computerised rides, a wave machine and swimming pools.

In the geographic centre of Bahrain, standing alone in the desert about 2 km (about 1.2 miles) from Bahrain's only 'mountain', Jebel Dukhan, is a thorn tree known as the 'Tree of life'. This flourishing mystic tree provides shade from the heat of the day, although its source of water remains a mystery.

'Jebel Dukhan' translates into English as 'the mountain of smoke' because of the misty haze that surrounds it on hot and humid days. At 134 m (439.6 ft) above sea level, it is the highest point in Bahrain. A popular attraction for children was the pirate's cave, but this can no longer be visited as Jebel is occupied by the military, just like the southern region of Bahrain.

Major Festivals and Holidays

These are the major holidays and festivals celebrated in Bahrain:

- **Eid-al-Fitr**
  A two-day holiday taken on the first and second day of the Arabic month of Shawwal
- **Eid-al-Hajj**
  A two-day holiday taken on the tenth and eleventh day of the Arabic month of Dhul-Hijjah
- **Muharram (Ashoora)**
  A two-day holiday taken on the ninth and tenth day of the Arabic month
- **Mawlid-Al 'Nabi**
  A one-day holiday taken on the twelfth day of Rabi'al Awwal
- **National Day**
  Celebrations on 16 December.
- **Christmas Day**
  A one-day holiday taken on 25 December, according to the Gregorian calendar
- **Gregorian New Year**
  A one-day holiday taken on 1 January.

ABSORBING THE CULTURAL EXPERIENCE

If you want to absorb the cultural experience, there are a number of physical attractions to be seen. You can make a good start by visiting The National Museum built on reclaimed land and located on the Al Fateh Highway between Manama and Muharraq. Opened in 1998, there are eight exhibition halls covering archaeology, ethnology, natural history and the fine arts of Bahrain. The National Museum incorporates a 'Heritage Village', reflecting the architecture of the houses, buildings, lanes and alleys that used to exist. The National Museum has a café where you can enjoy light refreshments and a shop where you can buy handicraft products, jewels inlaid with natural pearls, books, films, postcards and other souvenirs of Bahrain.

The Sheikh Isa National Library at Muharraq is soon to be completed at a cost of US$ 33 million. The four-storey library will house some 250,000 titles plus heritage items. A large conference hall will be incorporated into the complex.

The Museum of Pearl Diving is one of the most important and historic buildings in Bahrain. Opened in 1937 by the former ruler Sheikh Hamad bin Isa Al-Khalifa, it derives its importance from being the building that housed the first law courts. In 1984, the building was converted to a traditional heritage centre encompassing the story of Bahrain and its people from past to present.

The Oil Museum, situated in the centre of Bahrain near Oil Well Number 1, is where oil was first discovered. It has a collection of drilling equipment, documents, old photographs plus a working model of an oil rig. The museum was inaugurated in 1992 to commemorate the 60th year of the discovery of oil in Bahrain, the first country in the Middle East to do so.

For those interested in religion, the Ahmad Al-Fateh Mosque, also known as the Grand Mosque, is open to the public without appointment, except during prayer times. When visiting the Grand Mosque, conservative dress should be worn.

The oldest mosque in Bahrain and one of the most ancient relics of Islam is the Suq al-Khamis or the Al-Khamis Mosque. Easily identified by its twin minarets, the exact date of its original construction is unknown but it is thought to be around AD 682, which makes it more than 1,200 years old. Located on Shaikh Salman Road, the foundation for the twin minarets are believed to have been laid in AD 692. The mosque has been rebuilt twice—once in the 14th century and again in the 15th century.

Bait Al Qur'an or Koran House comprises of a mosque, an auditorium, a library and a school. The house was purposely built to accommodate holy manuscripts and Qur'ans—a concept unique in the Gulf. There is an opportunity to learn more about Islam as lectures are given and many of them are open to the public.

Ad Diraz and Barbar Temples are ancient sites dating back to the second and third millennia BC and contains a sacred well and three stone-built temples. Excavations carried out in the 1950s and the 1960s revealed that the Barbar Temple was built as a place of worship to Enki, the God of Spring Waters.

Bab al Bahrain is the gateway to Bahrain. Built in 1945, under the direction of the former advisor to the ruler of Bahrain, it is an icon of Bahrain with Islamic features. Since its construction, it has been refurbished and is now the headquarters for the directorate of tourism.

Bait Jasrah or Al-Jasra House was built in 1907 by Sheikh Hamad bin Abdulla Al Khalifa and was the birthplace of the father of King Hamad, Sheikh Isa bin Salmon al Khalifa. The house was restored in 1986 and represents the traditional architecture of Bahraini houses. It is open to the public.

There are a number of forts reflecting Bahrain's past. The Qal'at Arad or Arad Fort located on the Island of Muharraq is quite close to the airport. It is probably one of the first landmarks you will see when you fly into Bahrain. The fort derives its name from Aradous, the Greek name for Muharraq. The fort is of Arab construction, rebuilt in the 16th century by the Portuguese and was used to counter local resistance, guarding the approaches to Muharraq Bay from pirates and precluding attacks from the Ottoman commander whose base was in Ehssa, Saudi Arabia. At one time, the Omanis occupied the fort. Recently, it has undergone extensive restoration using original materials including coral stone, lime, gypsum and date palm. The fort is open to the public and is now illuminated at night. It is also a venue for concerts.

Cottage industries such as basket weaving are still practiced by some of the people.

The capital city of Manama is developing rapidly as can be seen by the building cranes and construction sites in the background.

The modern and the traditional co-exist in harmony in Bahrain. Locals in traditional dress visit an American fast-food chain.

Men relax by smoking
tobacco at a local cafe.

Bahrain's mosques have beautiful domes and minarets reflecting the country's Islamic heritage.

Taking Pictures

It's generally OK to take pictures in Bahrain. Like in all other countries, you should not take photos of the military and other security installations. It is considered bad taste to take photos of Bahrainis without their permission. There is a print ad that invites visitors to email their pictures to them at their email address at bahrain@newarabia.net.

On Muharraq Island, there is also the Qal'at Abu Mahir, sometimes known as the Abu Mahir Fort. This fort was originally built in the 16th century and has been rebuilt several times. It currently stands on the grounds of the coast guard station.

Qal'at al Bahrain, also known as the Bahrain Fort, is the most prominent of the ancient fortifications. Prior to becoming a fort, the area contained residential dwellings thought first to have been constructed in 2800 BC. Over time, the settlement became fortified and at one stage, it was the palace of the Assyrian King Sargon. Later, the Portuguese built a fort in the 16th century to defend their acquisition of Bahrain. The Qal'at al Bahrain is also known as the Portuguese Fort. Some Bahrainis believe that the fort is haunted by ghosts or *jinns* who appear at night.

The Salman bin Ahmed Al Fateh Fort is one of the most significant forts in Bahrain. Originally built in the 17th century, the fort is located strategically on a low escarpment overlooking the valley between east and west Riffa, which is an ideal military location. A new fort was built on the ruins of the old fort in 1795. The new fort represented typical 19th century military architecture and included a mosque for the soldiers to pray in before battle.

Later, the fort became a private residence. More recently, the fort has been restored and is now open to the public. Exhibits include displays of religious documents, traditional trades and crafts and the reconstruction of a *souq* as it was in the 1930s.

Expat Clubs

Bahrain has approximately 30 clubs and associations, ranging from sporting clubs, company sponsored clubs, cultural clubs, service clubs, national clubs and business clubs. Bahrain is one of the most liberal countries in the Arabian Gulf and actually has 'ladies nights' and go-go shows. Many of the hotels provide entertainment and some bring in overseas artistes to perform in their discotheques. Many British expats are members of the British Club or the Dilmun Club, whose facilities include tennis courts, swimming pools and restaurants. Younger expats are usually more attracted to the Bahrain Rugby Club. The club attendance is highest over the weekends when games are actually played.

Those not wanting to go to a club often go to a hotel, where expat Bahrain residents who are not guests are allowed to use their facilities, including the swimming pool, gymnasium and spas, for a fee. Over the weekends, many of the hotels offer a buffet. Younger expats like to go to the English style pubs found at some of the hotels where they can enjoy a pint of draught beer and play darts.

Special Celebrations

If you are on the 'A' list, you might be invited to a presentation of Cartier's latest collection of jewellery at the residence of the French ambassador or invited by the chief executive of a prestigious hotel like the Ritz-Carlton to exclusive cocktail parties.

Other important events in the social calendar for expats include 'Burn's Night' for the Scottish expats, where the Bahrain Caledonian Society celebrates the occasion with a traditional Scottish dinner followed by a ball featuring traditional Scottish dancing.

There are more than 25 Indian associations and clubs in Bahrain. The Pongal harvest festival is an important event for Tamil expats. The festival is celebrated by the Tamil Cultural Association and by Tamil members of the Indian Club. The ceremony commences with the floors being decorated with intricate designs using *colam* powder. This is followed by a pot beautification ceremony, including the boiling of the cooking pot ritual. Then traditional songs are sung in accompaniment to music and there are traditional dances. The celebration also includes traditional games including *uri adithal*, tug of war and *kabaddi*. The feast itself is served on banana leaves.

The Lions Club Bahrain has drawing competitions for children. Other events include art exhibitions, public lectures and funfairs.

The *Gulf Daily News* has a page called 'Make a Date', which highlights social events that are happening in Bahrain. The other daily newspaper, *Bahrain Tribune*, lists social events in its 'Planner Column'.

Sports and Hobbies in Bahrain

Gulf Arabs are renowned for their love of horses and in Bahrain, this is no exception. The Arabian horse has existed as a breed for several thousand years. The history of every Arab mare was so important to the tribe that the Sheikh knew all the details of each animal as well as he knew the history of his own family. The Bedu believed that the horse was a gift from God created from mist and dust. There are a few stables in Bahrain with horses for all ages and riding skills. The Dilmun Club is a popular venue for expats.

Horse racing is popular in Bahrain. The first meet was held in 1942, where there was a tote and a proportion of the take was given to the war funds. In subsequent years, after the war, two or three meets were held on Fridays in the cooler months between October and March, with a part of the take from the tote given to the tuberculosis fund. Although the premier horse racing event in the Gulf is the Dubai Cup, Bahrain has an attractive grass-covered racecourse with an impressive grandstand and a seating capacity for 10,000 people. The Equestrian and Horse-Racing Club hosts meets every Friday in the cooler months. Like the rest of the Gulf, betting is now prohibited. Races are sponsored by commercial enterprises offering prize money ranging from 1,000–2,000 Bahraini dinars.

Camel racing is also popular in AGCC countries. Children from the sub-continent (India,

The top body for sport is the General Organisation for Youth and Sport.

Pakistan, Bangladesh, Afghanistan, Sri Lanka) are often used as jockeys. Human rights groups and the US State Government have raised concerns over the exploitation of small children by traffickers who pay impoverished parents a pittance or kidnap their victims. Qatar has addressed the problem by using robots as jockeys.

Soccer is probably the sport that most Bahrainis play and like to follow. There is a national sports stadium with a grass soccer pitch and an athletic track. The Bahrain national team competes in a competition comprising of other AGCC countries plus Yemen for the Gulf Cup. The winner of the Gulf Cup qualifies to compete in the Asian Cup. The Bahrain Football Association (BFA) is responsible for the Bahrain Premier Division Soccer League comprising of eight teams whose games are televised and broadcast over the radio.

Golf, a sport popular with expats is just beginning to be popular with Bahrainis who have the option of playing on a conventional golf course with fairways and greens or a uniquely Middle Eastern golf course. Features include driving from a tee placed on a hand-carried mat down a fairway made from a sand dune that has been levelled, and putting on browns made from sand smeared with a bitumen solution.

Bahrain has one championship standard 18-hole green golf course situated in the Riffa valley. The Riffa Golf Club is ranked as one of the top three golf courses in the Middle East offering both individual and corporate membership. In 2004, the annual subscription for corporate membership was 2,800 Bahraini dinars and 1,350 Bahraini dinars for individual membership. Visitors may also play at the golf club just by paying a fee of 36 Bahraini dinars for 18 holes. The Riffa Golf Club has a resident professional and there is the Golf Academy that conducts golf clinics in which they teach people how to play the game. The Club is managed by Gleneagles, a worldwide golf course management company.

Other Golf Clubs in the Region

Other top golf courses in the Middle East include the Doha Golf Club in Qatar as well as three others in Dubai, within the UAE: the Emirates Golf Club, the Dubai Creek Golf and Yacht Club and the Montgomerie Golf Club.

Golf in the Middle East is becoming increasingly popular and there is a belief that it will eventually replace Portugal and Spain as the popular destination for European golfers.

One of the oldest golf courses in the Middle East is the Awali Golf Club formed in 1939. Set in the desert, it is a traditional Middle Eastern golf course where members drive on sand fairways and put on browns.

Bahrain hosted its first international tennis event, the ITF Futures Championship in 2004, offering cash prizes of up to US$ 10,000. The tournament attracted a number of overseas entrants whose world ranking ranged from 294–998. The Bahrain Tennis Federation has courts at Isa town and the Bahrain Tennis Club has courts at Juffair. At both centres, the number 1 court has a seating capacity for 700 spectators.

Bahrain's original economic survival was based on diving for pearls. These days, recreational diving is a popular sport with water temperatures ranging from 34°C (93.2°F) in summer to 20°C (68°F) in winter. The recreational diver can observe more than 200 species of fish, explore the coral reefs and the wrecks that lay on the sea floor.

For those interested in boating, there is the Marina Club in Manama and the Bahrain Sailing club on Sitra Island.

In the major event sporting category, Bahrain is in the Formula 1 motor racing circuit and markets itself as the

regional hub for motor sports. Bahrain was one of the first countries in the Middle East to establish a motor racing club in 1952.

In April 2004, Bahrain hosted its first Formula 1 Grand Prix and is the first Grand Prix to be held in the Middle East. How was Bahrain able to secure the holding of the Formula 1 Grand Prix? Some Bahrain watchers have said that it was because Bahrain permitted the advertising of tobacco products.

The staging of the Grand Prix has bought significant economic benefits to the country. It has provided employment to 1,500 workers to complete the US$ 150 million project. The Bahrain International Circuit (BIC) is unique because it contains a 1,200 m (3,937 ft) drag strip, the first in the Arabian Gulf region which can be used for local and regional events. The circuit itself has four other tracks that can be used for regional and local events. It is planned that the Grand Prix track, which is 5,411 m (17,752.6 ft) long is to be used for other international events. There is also a circuit dedicated to the testing of new cars. Buildings on the Grand Prix circuit include five grand stands, plus an eight-storey VIP tower. Other buildings include a medical centre and media centre for some 500 local and international reporters who covered Bahrain's first Grand Prix in 2004.

Motor sports are becoming increasingly popular in the region, with the UAE rally being the second most important event in the region. Drivers from Qatar are making a bid to dominate rallying by competing in the Paris-Dakar rally.

Cricket is played in Bahrain but most of the participants are Western or sub-continental expats. The Bahrain Cricket Association's Premier Division has six clubs. Sharjah in the UAE hosts a major international cricket competition.

Other popular sports include coursing hares with silugi hounds and volleyball.

Despite the fact that most of Bahrain is a desert, there is a Bahrain Garden Club where many Western expats can pursue horticultural interests such as the growing of vegetables in plots allocated to them. The club also arranges for horticulturalists to give lectures to members on ways to improve their ability to grow vegetables in Bahrain.

Royal Falconry

Falconry is an aristocratic sport in Bahrain, indulged in only by the ruling family. The two breeds used for hunting are the *Peregrine* and *Saker* falcons. The *peregrine* falcon is the fastest bird in the world diving at up to 300 kmph (186.4 mph), punching the prey with its talons, knocking it to the ground. The falcons quarry includes the Houbara Bustard, the Stone Curlew and desert hares. It takes about two weeks for a good Arab falconer to train a year-old falcon and nearly a month to train a falcon that is two to three years old. The falcon is an important symbol in Bahrain, being the emblem displayed on the tail of the Gulf Air aircraft and is the name of their first class lounge.

Dubai is generally regarded as the sporting capital of the Middle East, whose major events include the Dubai Cup (the richest horse race in the world), the Dubai Desert Classic Golf Tournament, the Dubai Tennis Open, Class One Powerboat Championships and the World Equestrian Games Endurance Race. All these events are for substantial prize money and attract international sporting celebrities.

The Arts

Bahrain's long history is associated with the sea. Local songs and dances have a strong maritime flavour, associated with pearling and fishing themes. Bahrain has an arts culture involving poetry, storytelling, song and dance. The culture of Bahrain is usually displayed on special occasions. The National Council for Culture and Arts is the body responsible for nurturing and preservating heritage and culture.

The Bahrain Music Institute holds Western music concerts from time to time at its premises in Mahooz.

Architecture

Traditional Arab architecture is reflected in houses, mosques and the marketplace. Although each country in the Arabian Gulf has its own style in building design, there are common traits. Middle Eastern architecture is

characterised by arches, domes, minarets and towers with calligraphy in Arabic or intricate geometrical carvings on external surfaces.

Privacy and climate are important considerations in the design of houses. Windows are small and are often covered with a decorative wooden grill. Doors are a feature of the architecture and are often beautifully carved, and high walls surround the houses.

Bahrainis value their privacy and many houses have large locked gates with small shuttered or barred windows. Houses often have a shuttered balcony so that women who lived a restricted life could watch whatever was going on in the street below. There is only one door in the courtyard leading to the street. Rooms often face a central courtyard. There are separate quarters for men and women with each room having its own purpose and it is not possible to walk from one room to another.

Most mosques are built around a courtyard and have domes or minarets, although some have neither because the community had insufficent funds.

Modern Bahrain architecture incorporates ideas of the past with those of the present. The Novotel al Dana is a classic example of a hotel that has been designed to resemble a Bedouin village.

An impressive example of 19th century Arab architecture is the Siyadi house, built by Ahmed bin Qassem, a pearl merchant. Features of the house include ornate ceilings, stained glass windows, carved screens and a room without windows with a large safe set into the wall where the merchant could count his money without being seen. The house also contains a small upper reception room plus a *majlis* or large meeting room where men could meet.

Another example of traditional Bahraini architecture is Sheikh Isa's house, who was King Hamad's great-grandfather. Located in the old town of Muharraq, an important feature of the house is the wind tower, the precursor to present day evaporative air conditioning. Traditional Bahrain houses were built to be as cool as possible in the hot weather. Many traditional Bahraini houses have tall wind towers. Open on all four sides at the top, they can catch the wind from any direction. The wind tower cooled the house by acting as a funnel caching the breeze, drawing it into the house over pieces of wet cloth hung over poles in its path. The cool air circulated around the house and at the same time allowed the release of hot air through a kind of chimney.

Cinemas

There are seven cinema sites in Bahrain, most of which are in regional shopping centres and have multiple screens. The cinemas show the latest Hollywood movies and the most recent films from Bollywood in India. Egyptian films are also screened. Like the rest of the world, young adults attend cinemas most frequently.

Theatre

There is no resident professional theatre in Bahrain. At regular intervals, plays and musicals are staged, usually at hotels or exhibition and convention centres featuring overseas actors, mainly from the UK.

Major companies operating in Bahrain including Gulf Air often sponsor the plays, musicals and operas like *The Barber of Seville*. Theatre groups from other AGCC countries also make appearances in Bahrain. The Laughter Factory, a leading name in comedy with venues in Qatar and the UAE, have sessions in night clubs in Bahrain.

TOURING OUTSIDE BAHRAIN

The Arabian Gulf is emerging as an increasingly attractive destination for holiday-makers, particularly from Europe, seeking the winter sun. Even the reclusive Kingdom of Saudi Arabia is cautiously experimenting with the beginnings of a tourist industry to boost its economy and encourage its own residents to stay at home rather than travel overseas. Small numbers of specially invited guests from selected academic institutions can come on closely supervised tours. Despite the relaxation of restrictions that allows academics to travel into Saudi Arabia without a sponsor, few people would want to tour the country today. Although Bahrainis are poor cousins to their Saudi neighbours and despite the existence of the King Fahd Causeway, there is little inclination to travel to Saudi Arabia other than on business. There are some expats living in Bahrain who travel to the eastern province of Saudi Arabia to work each day.

Bahrainis who can afford overseas travel usually head for the UK, US, France, Germany or Thailand. With general belt tightening and the high cost of travel to Europe and North America, regional travel has become attractive. Favourite destinations include the UAE and other Gulf states, followed by Egypt, Syria and Jordan.

LEARNING ARABIC

CHAPTER 8

'...a word of advice. You'll hear many people tell you
Arabic is difficult; they will try to discourage you from
using it. It's just as easy or difficult as any language...'
—From the booklet of spoken Arabic of the Gulf

SPEAKING ARABIC

Arabic is the official language of Bahrain although English is very widely spoken. Bahraini school students are taught English from an early age. Information including traffic signs and car number plates are in both English and Arabic. As a matter of courtesy to Bahrainis, you should be able to say a few words in Arabic.

Arabic, like most languages, has its regional spoken variations. The colloquial Arabic spoken in the Arabian Gulf countries is different from the Arabic spoken by Egyptians, Iraqis, Jordanians and Syrians. But these dialects are not so different that you will not be understood speaking Arabian Gulf Arabic in these countries, as the authors discovered when they visited Cairo. Egyptians regard the speaking of Arabian Gulf Arabic as quaint, but they certainly don't show it if you are a wealthy Saudi. The Arabic spoken in North Africa is different, causing more problems in comprehension.

The spoken Arabic of Bahrain is a direct descendant of the Classical Arabic of Arabia. The colloquial form of Bahrain Arabic has been simplified in structure and influenced by Persian, Urdu, Egyptian and English. Somewhat surprisingly, there are regional dialects in such a small geographical kingdom.

The English numerical system is based on the Arabic numerals. The development of computers has enhanced English as the principal business language, although Arabic, being an alphabetised language, can be typed on a 'qwerty' keyboard.

خفف
السرعة الآن
REDUCE
SPEED NOW

Information signs are in both Arabic and English.

Even in Bahrain, the colloquial Arabic is slightly different from other Arabian Gulf countries. The few foreign words incorporated into Arabic are mainly technological. For example, a car is *sayyaarah*. There are some interesting derivations. An aeroplane is a *tayyaarah*—the car that flies. Another English word incorporated into Arabic is the description of all meat as *laham* (lamb). In Egypt, there was no Arabic word for police but since the police then wore shorts, they became *shortiis*.

The Arabic alphabet consists of 28 letters, all consonants written from right to left. Some letters may be connected while others may not. Most letters have a special form when they stand as the final letter of a word. There is a method of indicating long vowels but short vowels are not normally indicated. If a vowel is incorrectly shortened or lengthened, the word can have an entirely different meaning. For example, *matar* with a short vowel is 'rain', whereas *mataar* with the long vowel is 'airport'. Some sounds in Arabic are quite strange to English-speaking people.

In Arabic, some sounds have a light form and others have a heavy form, which also sounds quite strange in English.

The Arabic Alphabet

Letter	Name	Transliteration
ا	alif	a
ب	bā	b
ت	tā	t
ث	thā	th
ج	jim	j
ح	ḥā	ḥ[2]
خ	khā	kh
د	dāl	d
ذ	dhāl	dh
ر	rā	r
ز	zā	z
س	sin	s
ش	shin	sh
ص	ṣād	ṣ
ض	ḍād	ḍ
ط	ṭā	ṭ
ظ	ẓā	ẓ
ع	'ain	'
غ	ghain	gh
ف	fā	f

Pronounciation Guide

Vowels

There are three short vowels:

- **a**   as in *pat*
- **i**   as in *pit*
- **u**   as in *put*

They are frequently pronounced so quickly that they become quite indistinguishable and hence are not very important.

There are three long vowels which are very important and must be given their proper quantity.

- **aa**   as *a* in *father*
- **ii**   as *ee* in *seed*
- **uu**   as *oo* in *moon*

Dipthongs

In spoken Arabic, the dipthong transliterated

- **ai**   as *ai* in *main*
- **au**   as *o* in *home*

A final **ah** and **uh** are often reduced to a short vowel like the final *e* in the Italian word *dente*.

Others Points to Note

The letter **k** is often pronounced like *ch* as in *chair* in Bahrain and is a result of Persian and Urdu influences, even though there is no sound of this kind in pure or classical Arabic. For example, *Kibriit* or *chbriit* is 'matches', *samak* or *samach* is 'fish'.

There is no indefinite article 'a' or 'an' so that *bait* can mean 'house' or 'a house' and *walad* can mean 'boy' or 'a boy'. The definite article 'the' is *al* and is attached to the beginning of the word so that *al bait* is the house and *al walad* is the boy.

There is no special construction in spoken Arabic when asking a question, it is indicated simply by the tone of the voice so that *yaruuh*, *as suug*, may mean 'he is going to the market' or 'is he going to the market?'.

The usual negative with the verb is *maa* or *muu* so that *maa faham* means 'he didn't understand' and *muu zain* means 'not good'.

There is no verb 'to have' in Arabic and this must be expressed by 'ind-' before a vowel or 'inda-' before a consonant meaning 'with' so that *indii* means 'with me'. 'I have' and *Indana* means 'with us we have'.

Arabic numbers are read from left to right. There are no capitals used at the beginning of words as in English. Classical Arabic as used in the Qu'ran is the only form of written Arabic. Spoken classical Arabic's grammar is more complex than colloquial Arabic. For those wanting to learn a few phrases, the authors recommend starting with the greeting. This will enable the exchange courtesies with Bahrainis in their own language.

To Keep In Mind

- Begin by learning the alphabet and paying particular attention to those sounds that are new and strange to English-speaking people. Next, learn the greetings.
- Some words have a wheezy sound like the noise you make when you breathe on glasses to clean them. Other words have a choking sound.
- If a vowel is incorrectly shortened or lengthened, the word may have a completely different meaning. For example, *matar* is rain but *mataar* is airport.
- Arabic words are either masculine or feminine so that not only persons but also things must be classified as 'he' or 'she'.

LANGUAGE SCHOOLS

There are schools teaching Arabic, but not many Western expats avail themselves of the opportunity as English is so widely spoken in Bahrain. There are also a number of institutions teaching other languages and a number of cultural organisations including Ecole Francais de Bahrein, the American Cultural and Educational Centre, Berlitz Bahrain and the British Council. The British Council's office in Bahrain is attached to the British Embassy. They engage in a number of activities promoting British culture including the sponsorship of popular musical groups such as Heart and Soul.

DOING BUSINESS
IN BAHRAIN

CHAPTER 9

'Bahrain is ranked the most economically
free country in the Middle East and is the
fourth most free economy in the world.'
—Heritage Foundation and *Wall Street Journal*

ALTHOUGH THE PRINCIPAL FOCUS OF THIS BOOK is on Bahraini customs and etiquette, the authors feel that the inclusion of a chapter on doing business in Bahrain is good background knowledge for visitors.

Bahrain used to have a reputation as a hardship posting, because the living conditions were poor. Up until the mid-20th century, most of the houses were built of coral stone quarried from the seabed, the streets were narrow and congested and the little shops with wooden shutters stocked few Western goods. Fish, meat and vegetables were sold in fly-infested matting booths. There was only one hospital in the capital, roads in the town were unpaved and those in the country were nothing more than desert tracks.

Carried Ashore

When Lord Curzon, the then Viceroy of India, visited Bahrain in 1901, he arrived on a ship that anchored 5 km (3.1 miles) off the coast and was transferred in a skiff which ferried him to the shore. As there was no pier, he was carried ashore from the skiff in a chair to which poles had been attached.

All this has changed. Bahrain has a modern airport, the standard of housing is equal or superior to most cities and towns in the West and there is an extensive network of roads and highways.

Modern supermarkets and department stores stock a wide range of products and there is a high standard of education and healthcare.

ECONOMIC HISTORY OF BAHRAIN

Before the discovery of oil, the principal economic activity of Bahrain was pearling. Pearls, according to the Qu'ran, were the property of paradise. Bahrain was the greatest source of pearls in the world and became the centre of the pearling industry in the early 19th century. Bahraini pearls have an unusual lustre, thought to occur because of its environment that is made up of nurtured fresh water springs bubbling to the surface to mix with sea water, coupled with the hard sub-strata of the ocean floor.

Bahrain was known as the Pearl of the Gulf. A landmark in Bahrain is the Pearl Roundabout, built to commemorate the formation of the Arabian Gulf Cooperation Council (AGCC). Many buyers travelled to the international pearl markets in Bombay (known as Mumbai today) and Baghdad. The history of pearls in the Arabian Gulf can be traced back to the Stone Age. Local legend has it that when pearls were crushed and consumed, they provided eternal life. Believing this to be true, King Gilgamesh from Urak in Mesopotamia sent ships to the Arabian Gulf to seek out the pearl fields.

Some 4,000 years ago, a pearl set in a gold earring was excavated in Bahrain. Alexander the Great's admiral wrote in glowing terms of the world famous Bahraini pearls with their unmatched lustre.

In 1845, the Dawasir Arabs came to Bahrain where they became rich and powerful through ownership of a fleet of pearling *dhows*. The many divers on the *dhows* virtually worked as slaves.

The Bahrain Pearl Fleet was able to stay at sea for long periods because they could access fresh water by lowering leather pipes from the pearling *dhow* to the fresh water springs

Dhows

The word *dhow*, used to describe Arabian sailing ships, is actually an Indian word and in Arabic, boats are known by their individual names, such as *Boom Sambuk* and *Jalibut*, which were some of the boats seen sailing on the Arabian Gulf.

The Pearl Roundabout, a landmark that symbolises Bahrain's history of producing the finest pearls in the world.

on the seabed. The pressure from the springs made it possible to pump water up on to the deck of the *dhow*.

In its heyday, there were approximately 20,000 pearl divers working from a fleet of approximately 1,000 *dhows*.

The commodore of the pearling fleet was the *nakhuda*, appointed by the ruler. These days, the captain of a *dhow* is also known as the *nakhuda*. The commodore of the pearling fleet decided when the fleet would sail to the pearl banks, how long they would stay, and arranged for the sale of the pearls to a pearl merchant known as a *tawwash*, when the fleet returned to port. The *tawwash* in turn, sold the pearls to an international dealer. The pearling season, called *Al Ghaws*, was from May to September. The pearling *dhows* (*sambuks*) were of various sizes. Small pearling *dhows* had a small crew, whereas larger vessels had up to 80 men on board. The crew consisted of divers and pullers who pulled up the divers and rowed the *sambuk* on the last leg of the journey to the pearl banks or when there was not enough wind. Other members of the crew were a couple of ship boys, a musician, the captain's mate and the captain. The crew rowed to the accompaniment by a musician known as a *nahlan*.

The pearl divers, when working, wore only a pair of dark coloured shorts and a thin cotton suit to protect them from being stung by jellyfish. It was thought that bright coloured clothing might attract dangerous fish. They also wore leather guards on their fingers and toes to protect them from sharp shells. Their equipment also consisted of a nose clip made out of turtle shell.

It was illegal to use modern diving equipment as it was felt that the richer merchants who could afford the equipment would have an unfair advantage. Each diver had two ropes. One rope was weighted with a stone, enabling the diver to descend to the seabed quickly. The other rope was used to collect the oyster shells. A heavy stone or lead weight was attached to the diver by a line to make sure that he was not carried away from the *dhow* by the strong currents.

The divers made ten dives and then had a rest. The divers ate one meal a day in the evening and during the day, consumed small quantities of coffee. Divers were not paid regular wages but shared in the profit from the sale of the pearls. They did receive an advance at the beginning of the pearling season and again during the off-season. There was no shortage of men wanting to become divers because of the advance payment system coupled with the potential income from the sale of the pearls, which meant that they always had cash. What divers overlooked was that the cash advances were actually loans that had to be repaid later, with interest. The system ensured that the *nakhuda* always had sufficient divers because they were forever in his debt. The *nakhuda*, in turn, also borrowed money from a pearl merchant to provision his *dhow*. All charges incurred by the *nakhuda* from the pearl merchant, including interest, were passed on to the divers.

Pearl merchants from Manama and Muharraq regularly visited the pearling *dhows* in their luxurious launches and bargained with the *nakhudas* to buy the pearls. The split of profits was 20 per cent to the *nakhuda* and the balance to the divers. Unfortunately, the system was open to abuse with excessive rates of interest, falsified records and anything but transparent transactions.

Pearls were valued according to their shape, size, colour, lustre and number of imperfections. A very large pearl was sold separately whereas smaller pearls were sold by weight. The pearls were wrapped in a red cloth known as an *egmesh* and stored in wooden boxes. World War I triggered a downturn in pearl exports and the onset of the Depression in the 1930s coupled with the Japanese development of cultured pearls, brought the industry to an abrupt end.

WHO DOES THE REAL WORK?

Bahrain, like other AGCC countries, has indigenous workers plus a large expatriate workforce. Some expats may not be able to identify some of the people from the expatriate workforce, especially Arabs from Lebanon, Egypt and the Palestinian territories who have the advantage of speaking Arabic and have a greater understanding of Bahraini culture. Interestingly, those who speak Arabic are not perceived to be expatriates the same way Westerners, Asians and those from the sub-continent (India, Pakistan, Bangladesh, Sri Lanka, Afghanistan) are. There are virtually no expat guest workers from the AGCC countries of Kuwait, Oman, Qatar, Saudi Arabia and the UAE.

Most guest workers in Bahrain come from Bangladesh, India, Pakistan or Sri Lanka. Other Asian guest workers are from the Philippines, Thailand and Korea. Western expat guest workers tend to come from the UK, US and Australia.

The first significant influx of guest workers came to Bahrain following the discovery of oil. They were employed to build the refinery and when this was completed before

World War II, it was one of the largest in the world. Other guest workers were employed to build infrastructure projects associated with the development of the oil industry. While Saudi Arabia and the other Arabian Gulf states completely relied on guest workers to build their infrastructure when oil was found, Bahrain employed guest workers and nationals to develop their infrastructure.

Western visitors arriving in Bahrain are often surprised that the chauffeur driving them in a limousine from the airport to their hotel is actually a Bahraini. Taxi driving is an occupation reserved only for Bahrainis. Unlike many of the Arabian Gulf countries, Bahrainis do work in the service sector in occupations such as being a hotel porter or as concierges in hotels. Bahrainis also occupy executive roles in banks, middle managers in multinational corporations and some are executive directors and chairmen of companies at the big end of town.

Bahrainis and guest workers were employed to work in a variety of occupations, the most recent being the hospitality industry. The finding of oil and the building of the refinery generated more funds to develop more infrastructure projects, requiring a larger labour force filled by expats and Bahrainis. There is still a large guest workforce made up of many nationalities but dominated by expats from the sub-continent who come and go, depending on the demand for labour. Bahrainis have a higher participation rate in the private sector than other nationals do elsewhere in the other Arabian Gulf countries. Bahrainis also work in a greater variety of occupations compared to their counterparts in Saudi Arabia and the UAE.

Occupations and organisations almost exclusively staffed by Bahrainis include the Bahrain Defence Force, the police and the civil service. Expats from the sub-continent tend to be technicians or be involved in retailing while expats from Asia tend to work in the service industries. According to the *Bahrain Tribune*, most Bahrainis prefer to work in the government sector because of job security.

A recent development has been the import of guest workers from Bulgaria to work in the hospitality industry.

THE PECKING ORDER

There is a fairly well defined pecking order in Bahrain, and your place depends on who you are, where you have come from and your job in Bahrain. At the highest level stands visiting royalty and there are many royal visits to Bahrain from rulers in the region. Visiting royals receive, on arrival, the red carpet treatment par excellence, with the full guard of honour and all the other trimmings accorded to a member of a royal family. By Western standards, it is a bit over the top, with excessive film footage and media coverage of the visiting royal meeting with the who's who of Bahrain society. The media accords the full title of the royal each time their name is mentioned.

Within Bahrain, the senior members of the great merchant families, with their connections to royalty, head the pecking order. Not far behind are the salaried workers of some importance, like ambassadors or the chief executive officers of multinational or leading Bahraini companies. Not quite so well up the pecking order are those that have come to work in a senior management role from a smaller Bahraini company or a middle management role in a larger organisation.

Further down the pecking order are those who work in clerical and service positions, who earn around 120 Bahraini dinars per month. As part of their contract, their employer provides them with free air travel to their place of recruitment every two or three years.

Where you come from also determines your place in the pecking order. Further down the pecking order are expat workers from the sub-continent in skilled and semi-skilled jobs, earning between 50–80 Bahraini dinars per month. They are overtly discriminated against by the Bahrainis and, to some extent, by Western expats.

Near the bottom of the pecking order but in much better financial shape are the call girls from Eastern European countries like Bulgaria, Romania and Asia who service the needs of the adult male Saudis.

On the bottom tier of the pecking order are the Bangladeshis, who mostly work as casual labourers hired on a daily basis. They can be seen sitting or standing on street corners, waiting for a job. When employers or companies want unskilled labour for a day's work, they send out a pick-up truck and, like cattle, they round up the Bangladeshis from the street and take them to the work site. At the end of the day, the pick-up truck deposits them back on the street.

Like the rest of the world, having the right connections helps you move up the pecking order. There is more than a grain of truth in the expression, 'It's not what you know but who you know'; except that in Bahrain and the Arabian Gulf, having the right connections is known as *wasta*.

EMPLOYMENT CONTRACTS

Before taking up employment in Bahrain, it is essential that you have a contract with your employer. The Bahrain law requires the employment contract to be registered with the government. Bahrain commercial law requires a company operating in Bahrain or a person sponsoring an employee to pay a reasonable salary or wage, provide suitable accommodation and provide the employee with free travel back to his place of recruitment. Recently, the government announced changes in the sponsorship rules, making it much easier for guest workers to change sponsors, giving more flexibility to the job market. Employment contracts for managers working for international corporations with an operation in Bahrain are not so much legal documents but more like a letter of appointment, spelling out the remuneration package. Executives working for Bahraini companies may actually have a formal contract, setting out the conditions of employment.

The length of the employment contract varies and with many guest workers from the sub-continent, it is often automatically renewed if they have given satisfactory service and if there is a job for them to do. Employment contracts for non-executive guest workers in the hotel industry are usually for two years, with home leave every year. As Bahrain has a large number of public holidays, lower income guest workers do not usually have local leave. Contracts for senior managers in some major Bahraini companies are for a period of up to three years. The government does permit a period of 2–3 months for employers to lodge a new employment contract after the previous contract has expired.

Many major corporations engaging managerial staff often fly the candidate executive and their spouse to Bahrain before taking up the appointment, so that they can observe the culture and what it is going to be like to work and live in Bahrain. Those undertaking a pre-assignment trip should make a particular point to evaluate accommodation options as there is a good supply of houses and apartments. Which district to live in, the available recreational options and the type of schools available for their children are some other things to consider.

The remuneration package for managers has often been constructed with input from a human resources firm, specialising in remuneration packages for international managers. The package usually consists of a base salary equivalent to what the position would pay in the home country plus a foreign service allowance to reflect the relative hardship of living in Bahrain and the different cost of living to the home country of the manager. The expat allowance has to reflect the increased cost of living in Bahrain. Western expat managers get up to 20 per cent of their base salary to reflect the cost of living differential and the hardship allowance is up to 15 per cent of their base salary. With the globalisation of managerial positions, there has been a worldwide trend for the foreign service component of the remuneration package to decline. There is an increasing trend of determining salaries paid to managers working overseas by market forces.

In addition to base salary and foreign service allowances, fringe benefits for managers working in Bahrain usually include free or subsidised housing, a company car and a recreational allowance. The recreational allowance is to cover the fees associated with membership of a sporting or country club. Some of the five-star hotels offer the use of their swimming pool, gymnasium and other recreational facilities to residents in Bahrain who are not guests. They pay a fee and become members of the hotel's club.

Major corporations usually pay the school fees of manager's children in Bahrain or boarding school fees if they are being educated in their home country. Larger companies usually pay the airfares of the manger's children to visit their parents if they are at school in their home country.

The letter of appointment often includes the frequency, duration and class of travel for home leave for the manager and his family. For guest workers on managerial status, there may be a leave component allowing the family to travel in the region. Jordan has become a popular destination for Western expats living in the Arabian Gulf.

In medium to smaller companies, any ambiguities in the employment contracts of junior employees from the sub-continent or Asia are likely to be exploited in favour of the Bahrain employer. Resolution of labour disputes can be long drawn out affairs because of the involvement of the Ministry of Labour and Social Affairs and the justice system, which both work independently of each other.

Making a Case

The *Bahrain Tribune* reported the case of Danny D, a 36-year-old fashion designer, who in 2002 filed a case of non-payment of five months salary. The Ministry ruled in his favour but his employer appealed the case to the law courts. Danny considered himself more fortunate than some other litigant guest workers because the court had given him permission to continue working in Bahrain while his case was being heard. Other guest workers from the sub-continent or Asia have not been so fortunate. The *Gulf Daily News* reported a case involving 15 Indian hotel workers who claimed that they had not been paid for up to one year and have had to live off the charity of friends. When the Ministry of Labour and Social Affairs set a date to hear the case, management from the hotel failed to turn up and the case was postponed.

Despite occasional disputes, Bahrain has probably got one of the best commercial legal systems in the Arabian Gulf because it is based on British commercial law that is based on precedent.

A number of Filipino workers caught in labour disputes have had to overstay their contract without income in Bahrain because of the delay in time taken by the Ministry of Labour and Social Affairs in hearing their cases. Even if the Ministry of Labour and Social Affairs rules in favour of the guest worker, there can be delays as the Bahrain employer has the right and usually does appeal the Ministry's decision to the law courts. In some instances, guest workers have been in litigation for up to three years and felt trapped. The delays occur because the law courts act independently of decisions made by the Ministry of Labour and Social Affairs. When a case comes before the law courts it has to be heard again from the beginning, making it expensive, time-consuming and frustrating for the employee litigant. Most labour disputes are related to the alleged non-payment of wages and other emoluments by the employer to a relatively low-paid guest worker from the sub-continent or Asia.

ECONOMIC OVERVIEW

The *Heritage Foundation* and the *Wall Street Journal* judged Bahrain to be the freest economy in the Middle East and the fourth most free in the world.

Bahrain is geographically the smallest of the AGCC countries but is one of the leading commercial centres in the Middle East. Bahrain has had in place, over the last 20 years, a developed infrastructure together with good education, health and municipal services. These are being constantly improved. Bahrain, along with Dubai, is one of the best places for expats to live in the Middle East. Some expats say Bahrain is a better place to live than Dubai because of its lower cost of living. Bahrain is an excellent location to make contacts in the Middle East for multi-national corporations and in particular, those in the banking sector.

Bahrain is solidly prosperous, although its highest rate of economic growth was in the 1970s and the 1980s when oil prices were high. In the 1990s, Bahrain began losing its status as the hub of the Gulf region to the UAE and Dubai in particular. In 1995, the economy further contracted as a result of political disturbances.

Like Dubai, Bahrain is much less dependent on oil than the other Gulf States. Bahrain has carved a niche outside the oil industry by attracting US$ 85 billion in offshore banking assets, having a skilled workforce, excellent communications and a regulatory system considered the best in the region. Bahrain, having established itself over the last three decades as the region's pre-eminent international financial centre, is lobbying to become the regional headquarters for an anti-money laundering body for the Middle East and North Africa.

Many years ago, Bahrain diversified into aluminium refining, ship repairs, petrol-chemicals and as a tourist destination for Saudis who can drive across the King Fahd Causeway to avail themselves of pleasures denied at home.

There is significant construction going on in Bahrain, as a result of seven major industrial projects. According to some observers, this has come about as a result of the 11 September incident. They say that Arabs who had money in US bank accounts became concerned that their funds would be frozen. To avoid this, they withdrew their funds and deposited the money in banks in Bahrain because it is a major international banking centre for offshore banking.

Saudis also like to invest their funds in Bahrain because they obtain higher interest rates than in Saudi Arabia.

Like the other AGCC countries, Bahrain's economic model is a high degree of central planning and state capitalism. In moving to shore up the economy and stimulate growth, the rules governing foreign investment were liberalised and the government introduced incentives to stimulate investment in the private sector. The Bahrain Government is keen to sell off some of its assets to the private sector to reduce its financial burden and to take on more of a role as a regulator rather than as an operator of businesses. A candidate for privatisation is the Eastern Power Station project, where it is estimated that electricity output will be doubled by 2020 through transferring ownership from government to a corporation.

The key sectors of Bahrain's economy are banking, tourism and service industries. Bahrain is now emerging as a regional centre for marketing communication and advertising firms.

GDP and Revenue

According to the United Nations World Bank IMF report, Bahrain has enjoyed the second highest long term GDP growth rate in the region on a per capita basis. Over the period 1975–2000, GDP per person grew at slightly less than 2 per cent. Oman had the highest rate of growth and the UAE had the lowest rate of growth. In 2001, government revenue was US$ 18 billion and outlays were US$ 22 billion.

The major long-term economic problems are the depletion of oil and underground water resources. Most of the water consumed in Bahrain is desalinated seawater or brackish underground water where salt has been removed.

The change of regime in Iraq has presented business opportunities for Bahraini companies. The US Government has been meeting with the Bahrain Chamber of Commerce and Industry to discuss prospects for Bahraini investors to participate in the reconstruction of Iraq. Announcements have been made regarding Bahraini and Iraqi joint ventures in the car market.

Oil and Bahrain

In 1932, oil was struck at Well Number 1 near Jebel Dukhan, making Bahrain the oldest producer of oil in commercial quantities on the western side of the Arabian Gulf. Bahrain commenced exporting crude oil in 1934. In 1935, work started on the construction of the Bahrain Petroleum Company's (BAPCO) refinery and an important economic milestone was marked by the completion of the first stage of the refinery in 1937. At that time, the Bahrain refinery was the fourth largest in the world.

The timely finding of oil in commercial quantities was a godsend to the Bahrain economy as it coincided with the collapse of the global pearl market, which had been the mainstay of the Bahrain economy.

Bahrain, like Oman and Saudi Arabia, has a fairly low oil income when measured on a citizen per capita basis. However, Bahrain, unlike most other countries in the region, is not dependant on oil for its economic prosperity. Like the Emirate of Dubai, oil exports in 2004 accounted for less than 15 percent of their GDP.

Although Bahrain does not have much oil or gas when compared to its neighbours nowadays, there is nonetheless an economically significant refinery generating approximately 60 per cent of Bahrain's external receipts, 60 per cent of government revenue and 30 per cent of GDP. The

Bahrain was the first AGCC country to strike oil and it looks like it will be the first country to run out.

refinery is dependent on receiving most of its crude oil from Saudi Arabia. The refinery is undergoing an upgrade estimated to cost between US$ 600–900 million and in addition to improving the quality of the finished product, output will be increased.

Today, many of the oil wells in Bahrain are concentrated near the highest point of the main island at Jebel Dukhan. In 1999, output of crude oil was 37,000 barrels per day. The Bahrain government has 60 per cent of the equity in the Bahrain oil field and now owns 100 per cent of the Bahrain Petroleum Company.

Recently, the ownership of an offshore oilfield between Bahrain and Saudi Arabia became controversial. Rather than enter into a dispute, the Saudis gave the oilfield to Bahrain.

The Bahrain and Indian governments have been in discussion regarding the setting up of a joint venture for value added petroleum products.

Economic Drivers

In both Bahrain and Dubai, there are large aluminium smelters powered by natural gas. Aluminium Bahrain (ALBA) operates a smelter plant close to the oil refinery on the east coast. Iron ore and bauxite are imported to make pellets. The Bahrain and Indian Governments have been discussing the viability of a joint venture to produce downstream aluminium products.

Bahrain also has a number of light industries. They include the manufacture of disposable hospital equipment, bedding, soft drinks, chemicals, furniture paint and paper products.

Bahrain is the financial service centre for the Middle East and a pioneer in Islamic banking whose charter is to contribute to the development of Islamic products and capital markets, and only invest in companies conforming to Islamic principles and conforming to Shari'a law. Around 80 per cent of Islamic banking transactions in the Arabian Gulf region are based in Bahrain. With sophisticated global communications, it services both regional and international customers.

There are 182 licensed financial institutions in Bahrain. They include 19 commercial banks, two specialised banks, 45 offshore banking units, 32 investment banks and 41 representative offices. In addition, there are 26 money exchangers, seven brokerage houses plus ten investment and financial consultant offices. Approximately 5,000 Bahrainis are employed in the financial sector. Bahrain's Islamic banks do not charge interest or derive wealth from what they consider improper sources. For example, they will not lend to companies whose products including alcoholic beverages or tobacco. Among the products offered by Islamic banks is the *sukuk*, a bond-like product. Since the 1990s, there has been significant growth in the demand for Islamic financial products and it is estimated that Islamic products finance around one-third of the market in the areas of banking, mortages, equity funds and derivatives.

For banks, Bahrain is located in a suitable time zone, has a stable currency, is a major regional deposit-taking centre and offers lending opportunities to businesses. Bahrain banks offer higher interest rates than in Saudi Arabia. This has left Saudi Arabia with a cash shortage as Saudis are borrowing money from their own banks at relatively low interest rates and depositing the cash in Bahraini banks where they receive a higher interest rate.

There is also a sophisticated insurance sector including *takafuls* (Islamis insurance firms), whose products conform to Islamic principles. Because of the relatively small Bahrain market, there are insurance companies who are forming strategic alliances with banks to market their products known as 'bancassurance'. The banking industry is regulated by the Central Bank of Bahrain.

In 1989, the Bahrain Securities Exchange was established. There are approximately 50 companies listed on the exchange grouped into banks, investment, insurance, services industries and hotels. Their longer-term plan is to list foreign companies. There are 14 official stock exchanges in the Middle East with stocks surging in 2004.

Ship repair and boat building are important industries. Traditional boats built include *dhows* and a traditional Bahrain craft—the *huwairiyah*, made only from date palm stems tightly bound together with date fibre and soaked in fish oil for waterproofing. *Dhows* are still made on the outskirts of Manama at Budaiya, near the King Faisal Highway and are open to the public. Modern vessels are constructed and repaired at the dry docks built on reclaimed land on Muharraq Island. The completion of the King Fahd Causeway dramatically boosted the number of Saudi tourists visiting Bahrain. In 2004, there were approximately two million arrivals, generating an income of US$ 288 million.

Bahrain has a small agricultural sector. Around 3 per cent of the land is considered arable and a further 6 per cent is used for meadows and pasture. The main crops are fruit and vegetables grown in the north of Bahrain Island, near the springs and freshwater aquifers.

Bahrain also has a few poultry and dairy farms. There are approximately 145,000 cattle, 590,000 sheep and 400,000 goats. The main problems facing Bahraini farmers are desertification and the rapid depletion of water.

Fish has always been an important item in the Bahraini diet. Approximately 38,000 tonnes of fish are caught each year from 450 fishing boats using traditional methods including nets and traps. Species of fish caught include hamour, shrimp, tuna, barracuda mackerel, snapper and

shark. A study by the Bahrain Centre for Studies and Research (BCSR) into the fishing industry indicated that the number of fishermen had declined by a third from 4,200 in 1998 to 2,940 in 2004 because of poor economic returns and shortages of some species of fish.

Traditional arts and crafts are still practised in Bahrain. Basket weaving can be seen in the village of Karbabad, close to the Bahrain Fort in the Seef district. Basket weavers usually sit outside in the shade of trees working with their split lengths of palm. Pottery is made in the village of A'ali, and mats for use in mosques and homes are made in the village of Sitra. The mats are made from a kind of grass called *aseel*, grown close to the sea.

The centre for cloth weaving is the Bani Jamrah Weaving Workshop at Budaiya, where cloth for ladies' cloaks and men's sarongs is woven. At one time, there were over 100 establishments weaving cloth. Bahraini women embroider *bischts* and other national dress in the village of Sanabis.

THE BAHRAINISATION PROGRAMME

Over half of the total workforce is made up of expatriate manpower. In 1998, the government initiated a programme to create 30,000 new jobs for Bahraini nationals. The Ministry of Labour and Social Affairs has developed career and vocational training programmes financed through the Training Levy Scheme. They also recently established the Commission of Career Development, whose mission is to increase the salaries of Bahrainies working in the private sector. An outstanding example of where the Bahrainisation programme has been successful is with the Bahrain Telecommunication Company (BATELCO), where, in 2003, 95 per cent of the workforce was Bahraini. Although most employees of BATELCO are Bahrainis, many of the employees of companies that they outsource to are staffed by expats.

Overall unemployment is low because of the large number of expats in the workforce but it is high amongst young Bahrainis. According to *The Economist* magazine, unofficial data revealed that unemployment amongst 18 to 30-year-old Bahrainis was 14 per cent in 2002. The Bahrain Institute of Banking and Finance (BIBF) has recommended that companies wanting to employ expats should be charged a fee by the government. The less skilled the expat worker, the higher the fee should be. The BIBF also recommended in 2004 that a fee of 1,200 Bahraini dinars be paid by employers wanting to recruit an unskilled or semi-skilled expat worker. Those expat workers with a high school diploma or equivalent should pay 600 Bahraini dinars. The fee for expat university graduates or equivalent should be 100 Bahraini dinars but those with higher degrees or PhD equivalents should only pay 50 Bahraini dinars. The BIBF says that a similar scheme in Singapore has had considerable success.

Not everyone agrees with the BIBF. The Prime Minister of Bahrain believes that although 'Bahrainisation' is a priority, it should not be at the cost of expats. The Prime Minister expects economic development to be at a pace to accommodate Bahrainis and expats in the workforce.

BAHRAINIS IN THE WORKFORCE

The first Bahrainis to join the workforce were recruited by Standard Oil to build a road between the first oil well and the settlement where the oil company employees lived. The drilling of more oil wells and the construction of the refinery created more jobs for Bahrainis. The government, with its royalties from oil, was able to create more jobs in the public sector and raise the educational standards of Bahrainis.

BAPCO instigated an on-the-job training programme and sent talented Bahraini employees overseas for vocational training, allowing them to assume more responsible positions when they returned home. Bahrain, like all of the Arabian Gulf States, has a workforce where expatriates mainly work in the private sector and Bahrainis mainly work in the public sector an almost exclusive domain of nationals.

High Expectations

There is an expectation by many recent Bahraini graduates working in the private sector that their employer should pay them a high salary, give them time off to attend and pay for further courses in addition to the on-the-job training and be fast tracked into senior positions. Bahrainis are inclined to change their jobs more frequently or start their own businesses more oftten than those working in the private sector in the West.

What distinguishes the Bahrain workforce from other Arabian Gulf workforces is the significant number of Bahrainis working in the private sector at all levels and in all occupations. The Bahrain Government is actively encouraging the private sector to employ more nationals.

Reflecting the economic buoyancy of Bahrain, the workforce is expected to double by 2020. Despite a fast growing workforce, unemployment is looming as one of the most important social issues. Official government statistics show an overall unemployment rate of 5 per cent, with more males being unemployed than females. Unofficial statistics show that the highest unemployment occurs amongst young people, where it is estimated that 14 per cent of those between the ages of 18 to 30 cannot get a job. Bahraini graduates regularly demonstrate about the lack of jobs. Another key social issue is the disparity of income. In 2006, per capita annual income of Bahrainis was approximately US$ 20,000 but around 33 per cent of nationals, mainly Shi'a's, earned less than US$ 7,500.

Trade unions are permitted in the private sector and only in selected ministries in the public sector. Ministries with workers unions include Interior, Health, Electricity and Water, Pension Fund, Post Office and Works and Housing. The umbrella trade union organisation is the General Federation of Bahrain Trade Unions (GFBTU). In 2004, the GFBTU requested that legislation be drawn up to allow all Government employees to belong to a union. There are 40 unions in Bahrain.

RELIGION IN THE WORKPLACE

In everyday business life, religion comes into play. Meetings are not scheduled during prayer times. Larger companies like Gulf Air have a mosque incorporated into their offices. Smaller companies will have a prayer room.

The everyday Arabic language is full of religious sayings. When Bahrainis meet, they will end their greeting by saying *al Hamdu lillaah* ('Praise be to God'). On fare-welling each other, Bahrainis will most likely say *fii amaan illah* which means 'May God go with you'. The Arabic equivalent of 'maybe' or 'probably' is *inshallah* ('if it is the will of God'). Muslim workers argue that a secondary benefit of praying five times a day is that it gives them a break from the intensity of their work and they can return to their job intellectually refreshed and be more efficient.

During Ramadan, business slows down and Muslim employees work shorter hours. Because they cannot eat during the day, Muslim workers tend to be bleary-eyed and drowsy. Non-Muslims living in Bahrain do not have to fast during Ramadan but they must not eat, drink or smoke in public during daylight hours. Some hotels will serve meals in their dining rooms during Ramadan but others will only serve meals in the privacy of the guest's room.

GETTING A JOB

Jobs are advertised in the daily newspapers by companies themselves or through employment agencies. Most jobs advertised in the local newspapers are for non-managerial positions. Expats wanting a managerial or professional job in Bahrain often have to be transferred by their company or respond to advertised jobs published in newspapers or magazines in their home country or be headhunted by an executive search firm or network themselves into a job. Major international executive search and selection firms like Ernst & Young do have offices in Bahrain, and senior executive positions like the general director for the National Library or the chief executive officer of International Financial Organisations are often advertised in international magazines like *The Economist*.

Other Arabs, if they want to work in Bahrain, may be able to network their way in by having sufficient *wasta*. As in the West, to carve out a corporate career depends on to some extent who you know as well as what you know. Put simply, *wasta* is the clout you have, by who you know and its ability to open doors and generally short circuit official channels. Some large corporations employ a man whose specific task is to make sure that important newcomers, especially if they are Western expat senior executives, have plenty of *wasta,* like the Western expat senior executive whom the authors knew, who was able to jump the line for his medical appointment. But foreign workers should also beware of the small number of unscrupulous agents who lure mainly low-skilled Asian workers to Bahrain under false pretences.

SETTING UP A BUSINESS

The advantages of starting up a business in Bahrain include a simplified administrative and legal system, no corporate personal or withholding tax, no VAT or any form of sales tax on goods and services. There are no foreign exchange controls. Neither are there any customs duty on imported raw materials or semi-finished commodities brought in for further processing or machinery imported for the manufacture or re-export of products. Other incentives to locate a business in Bahrain include a strategic geographic position with a gateway to Saudi Arabia, the largest Arab market in the Gulf via the King Fahd Causeway, free access to other AGCC countries, and another 100 million consumers in the wider Middle Eastern region. Bahrain also has the advantages of sustained low inflation, a relatively high standard of living and a multilingual trained and efficient labour force at one-third of the cost of industrialised countries.

Historically, Bahrain and the other Gulf States have always required overseas companies operating in Bahrain to have a local partner to sponsor them. The Bahraini partner or sponsor can be a Bahraini company or a Bahraini national who must have at least 51 per cent equity in the enterprise. Bahrain is leading the way in economic liberalisation, allowing foreign companies in some instances to have 100 per cent foreign ownership of their Bahrain enterprise. Companies involved in technology, tourism and manufacturing services can generally be 100 per cent foreign-owned. Specific exemptions may be also given to information technology and telecommunication service companies, hotels, restaurants, healthcare and educational training organisations. Also exempt are companies involved in re-assembly, redistribution, commercial project development and management consultants.

To set up a business in Bahrain, it is necessary to deal with the Commercial Registration Directorate and the Company Affairs Directorate. They require the company to have its shares listed in the country of its incorporation for a minimun of three years and have a paid-up capital of, at the very least, 3.7 million Bahraini dinars with 100 shareholders. They must show the government the articles of association and there should be no restrictions on the transfer of shares. They must assign to their representative office in Bahrain the right to transfer shares, distribute dividends and financial reports. They must also show the government their audited financials.

The listing requirements for domestic companies are similar to setting up a business except that the listed company must comply with the new Commercial Companies Law, have a paid-up capital and sales revenue of half a million Bahraini dinars and show a net profit over the last two financial years. To be able to recruit staff, it is necessary to negotiate with the Directorate of Employment within the Ministry of Labour and Social Affairs. Under the Bahrainisation Programme, there are quotas for the number of nationals that must be employed in companies and also a quota on specific occupations.

Land Leases and Rentals

The cost of operating a business in Bahrain is lower than most countries in the Arabian Gulf. Long-term land leases of up to 50 years for approved industrial projects are available through the Industrial Areas Directorate of the Ministry of Commerce and Industry. Legislative Decree Number 28 sets out the obligations of the contracting parties. In 2004, the cost of leasing land was US$ 2.70 per sq m per year and the cost of leasing a factory with a hangar style structure was US$ 333 per sq m.

Premium office accommodation in downtown Manama or the Diplomatic Area ranges from US$ 550–1,000 per month, whereas medium range offices of 80–120 sq m can be leased from US$ 10–25 per sq m.

In addition to the normal commercial loan arrangements available to overseas companies, the Bahrain Stock Exchange offers equity financing and the Bahrain Development Bank (BDB) is Bahrain's primary financial development agency. The BDB offers short- and long-term composite loans to finance capital assets and a core portion of working capital, venture capital in the form of equity participation, equipment leases and export financing of products manufactured in Bahrain. The BDF will offer a loan of up to 500,000 Bahraini dinars per project with a flexible repayment schedule including a grace period of up to three years at competitive interest rates and bank fees.

The BDB also provides financial assistance to small and medium-sized projects. Borrowers need to satisfy the BDB with the viability of the project through an independent feasibility study conducted by an approved consultancy. The company should have a good credit rating, a management structure, proper accounting and the assets of the project should be insured. The project must be registered and licensed in accordance with Bahraini law. Specifically excluded are loans to purchase real estate refinancing of debt, the purchase of consumer goods and the financing of wholesaling or retailing.

If you are an overseas company, it is extremely important to do due diligence before appointing a Master Distributor or Agent because once appointed, it is very difficult to change. Nearly all businesses have email and the most advanced business communication systems but having direct contact and visiting the market will cement business relationships and alert you to new business opportunities.

MANAGING THE WORKFORCE

Bahrainis and the people of the Arabian Gulf tend to accept their lot in life far more than Westerners and Asians. In business, they do not seem to have that driving ambition to work hard and rise to the top. There are of course exceptions, as exemplified by the handful of great merchant families, some with a global empire and others with a regional empire.

If you are taking up a management role in Bahrain, it is important for you to understand that it is quite difficult if not impossible, to dismiss a Bahraini. When recruiting Bahrainis, it is a good idea to ask nationals already working for you what they think of the candidate. Bahrain is a fairly small place and people who play together might stay together in your company. First impressions often last forever. On the first day when new Bahrainis start work, make sure they are made to feel welcome.

Bahrainis do not like to perform tasks outside their job description and it is important that when you interview a candidate for a job, you go over very carefully what the job entails. Bahrainis like to know where they fit into the organisation and it is very important that they know their role, where to get help and conform to the chain of command so that they will not lose 'face', especially in public. Throughout

Do's and Don'ts at the Workplace

Do's

- During recruitment interviews, ensure that the candidate knows in detail what the job entails and where he or she fits into the organisation.
- When recruiting a new Bahraini employee, ask other people working for you what they think about the various candidates.
- Make sure your new employee feels welcomed.
- Let your Bahraini employees know that you value them. Keep them in the loop.
- Make sure your employee tells you the true status of a project rather than what you want to hear.
- Encourage your employees to phone and inform their clients if they are not able to arrive on time for their appointments.

Don'ts

- It is unwise to discuss politics.
- Do not use English slangs.
- You will lose the respect of the Bahraini employees if you criticise a Bahraini worker publicly.

their employment with your company, keep Bahrainis in the loop, make them feel part of the organisation and let them know you value them. The senior management determines office protocol in companies and it is no different in Bahrain. As a general observation, larger companies operating in Bahrain have a reasonable degree of informality. Although there has been a global trend for offices to adopt an open plan, Bahrainis still feel, as in the West, that office size is an important indicator of an executive's status. In the authors' opinions, Bahrainis generally make the best private sector employees amongst the AGCC countries.

However, a weakness amongst all employees in the Arabian Gulf including Bahrain is poor time management. The word *inshallah*, meaning 'if it is the will of God', is frequently used in response to a question. So if you ask Bahrainis when can they finish a report, make a presentation or attend a meeting at a specific time the response will almost certainly be *inshallah*—if it is the will of God. When asking about the status of a project, be aware that Bahrainis may be inclined to tell you want you want to hear rather than the true status of the project.

One Man's Meat is Another's Poison

When developing sales and marketing campaigns, it is a good idea to consult Bahraini employees for any cultural implications in the programme. In central Australia, there is a mountain now known by its aboriginal name—*Ulahru*, rather than the English name—Ayer's Rock. Emirate Airlines, when advertising Australia as one of their destinations, always refers to the mountain by its less popular English name because the popular aboriginal name sounds like a very rude word in Arabic.

Some years ago, the Bahrain Theatre Company put on the Gilbert and Sullivan light opera, *The Pirates of Penzance*. Their advertising poster depicted a pirate with a patch over his eye. No Bahrainis came to see the musical. Why? Because the former Israeli Defence Minister Moshe Dyan wore a patch over his eye and the Bahrainis thought that the light opera was extolling the virtues of the Israeli Defence Minister.

Bahrain is probably the only place in the Arabian Gulf where in the private sector, expat managers may actually be supervising nationals. Western expat managers need to use different managerial skills when they are managing Bahrainis. Although Bahrainis have been working for Western expats for a longer period than other AGCC countries, Bahraini pride remains an all-important issue.

An expat chief executive of a marketing firm indicated that her challenge was to instil in her workforce the importance of arriving at meetings on time. Also, if they were going to be late for unforeseen reasons, they should at least call their clients and let them know. When an employee leaves the company, try to find out the reasons.

Patience and persistence, rather than loud, forceful and threatening speech, is the way to manage. For under-performing employees, focus first on what they are doing well then calmly suggest how you would like to see things done in the future. A direct approach will usually be taken as a personal attack on the employee and will eventually be unproductive.

Board meetings in large Bahraini companies are often conducted in two languages, English and Arabic.

STAYING IN FAVOUR

Bahrainis are traditionally generous people and expats visiting or living in Bahrain should always be prepared to reciprocate in the exchange of gifts. Individuals should use their own discretion in accepting a gift from a Bahraini, bearing in mind the circumstance in which the gift is made, as it might be discourteous to reject an act of generosity.

Expats from the sub-continent working in large companies in supervisory positions often give relatively expensive gifts like Parker pens to the children of their Western expat boss. This causes some embarrassment to the boss but is done as a means

Gifts of Special Significance

After he attended a *majlis* at the Riffa Palace, the father of one of the authors received a gold Omega watch with a picture of the amir on the face from the ruler. This was in honour of him having lived in Bahrain for two decades. When it comes to giving gifts to royalty, the former amir, Shaikh Isa bin Sulman al Khalifa, gave the Prince and Princess of Wales an 18-inch-long golden jewel encrusted *dhow* valued at £ 500,000.

of showing 'face'. Business gift giving is a feature of doing business in Bahrain. Popular business gifts are ties, carpets and clocks. An unusual gift that can be purchased in the *souq* is an alarm clock in the form of a mosque, which when set, awakens you with Muslim prayers.

Some Bahrainis send Christmas cards to their Christian friends and this gesture may be reciprocated by sending cards on the two principal Islamic feasts Eid-al-Fitr and Eid-al-Hajj. If you do receive a Christmas card from a Bahraini, it should be acknowledged but it is not appropriate to send a Christmas card in return. In the case of the Royal Family, greetings should be expressed in person rather than by card.

EXPATRIATE WOMEN

One of the downsides of a man taking up a position in Bahrain is that it may be difficult for his wife to get a job of similar status to what she enjoyed in her home country. This is because of the 'Bahrainisation' programme that discriminates in favour of Bahrainis and requires the company that wants to employ an expat to prove that a Bahraini is not capable of doing the job. However, it is fairly easy for expat wives to find jobs as personal assistants, executive assistants, teachers and nurses.

As husbands are usually on relatively short contracts of one to five years, there are constant vacancies. If you are a woman recruited in Bahrain, you will receive a local salary rather than the expat remuneration package enjoyed by your husband. It is more difficult for expat women to get a managerial job, although the authors have met expat women who have been sales managers, entertainers, musicians and women working in the media; one of them was an expat woman who was the managing director of a marketing company. A good source of employment opportunities is from your country's chamber of commerce or diplomatic missions. Most expat women work for larger companies.

WHO IS IN BUSINESS?

As most businesses require a Bahraini sponsor or partner, all Bahrainis are potentially in business. The business

The Central Business District in Manama.

community in Bahrain includes affiliates of major trans-national corporations, large Bahraini companies with diverse business interests, sub-continental merchants and small to medium-sized businesses owned by Bahrainis and managed by nationals and expats.

Major corporations operating in Bahrain include the Bahrain Petroleum Company (BAPCO), Bahrain Telecommunication Company (BATELCO), Aluminium Bahrain (ALBA) as well as the Arab Shipbuilding and Repair Yard (ASRY).

The Bahrain Chamber of Commerce and Industry is the umbrella organisation representing business. There are also organisations like the Asian Traders Committee representing specific foreign business groups.

Unlike the UK, where the distinction between the Royal Purse and the government budget is transparent, in Bahrain they tend to merge. The Royal Family is also in business through loans or their sponsorships of foreign companies. More than 50 years ago, the Ruler of Bahrain made a loan to the fledgling Gulf Aviation Company to buy aircraft and spares from British Overseas Airways Corporation (now known as British Airways). Whilst the Royal Family does not overtly own businesses, they can be and are investors or sponsors of businesses which may have foreign partners. The King's sister is the sponsor of a medical related business. The ruling Khalifa family is the biggest landlord in Bahrain, owning all the best land in the archipelago.

Hussain Yateem had a passion for flying and was one of the first investors in the Gulf Aviation Company, the forerunner to Gulf Air. He loaned 2,000 rupees to the proprietor of Gulf Aviation (Freddie Bosworth) so that he could buy spare parts for his newly acquired Avro Ansen aircraft from Arabian American Oil Company (ARAMCO) in Saudi Arabia, who operated their own fleet of aircraft. Later, he became the first investor in the airline and today, the Yateem

Bahrain has an oligopoly of great merchant families whose origins can be traced back to when Bahrain was the pearl centre of the world. The discovery of oil in the 1930s facilitated their expansion into new business areas. The great merchant families include the Zayanis, originally pearl merchants who acquired the Arabian Gulf franchise for Land Rover and now has diverse business interests.

family has many business interests, including real estate and property development.

Mohammad Kanoo, a prominent merchant who was originally the General Sales Agent for BOAC, became the second investor in Gulf Aviation. Today, the Kanoo family has diverse business interests throughout the Arabian Gulf and is reported to be in the top 50 wealthiest families in the world.

Another investor in Gulf Aviation was Abdul Rahman Al Gosaibi. Today, the family's diverse business interests include retailing. Other Bahraini family companies with diverse business interests include Al Moyad and Fakro.

THE WAY AHEAD

Complimenting banking and finance, the Ministry of Labour and Social Affairs is promoting Bahrain as the regional centre for training and human resource management. Bahrain is also offering itself as the Middle East and North African regional headquarters for an anti-money laundering body.

The Bahrain Monetary Authority (BMA) is keen to make Bahrain a regional hub for insurance. Bahrain was the first country in the Arabian Gulf to introduce insurance and is the only country to offer an Arabic equivalent of the UK's Certificate of Insurance Practice.

The Economic Development Board (EDB) and the Ministry of Commerce and Industry are the main government agencies seeking overseas businesses to invest in Bahrain. They want Bahrain to become a knowledge-based economy focusing on health, IT and communications.

In 2004, Bahrain experienced a building boom with a skyline of cranes and bulldozers, creating a lot of dust. Major construction projects include the upgrading of the aluminium plant and oil refinery, a new container port, the Durrat al Bahrain Aqua Park, residential complex, and the Amwaj islands' smart city. Bahrain is also negotiating with Japan to build a car-making plant.

BAHRAIN AT A GLANCE

CHAPTER 10

'The Kingdom of Bahrain describes itself as a fully
sovereign independent Islamic Arab state whose
population is part of the Arab nation and whose territory
is part of the great Arab homeland. Its sovereignty may
not be assigned or any of its territory abandoned.'
—From the booklet *The Kingdom of Bahrain*

Official Name
Kingdom of Bahrain

Capital and Administrative Centre
Manama

Flag
The red and white flag of Bahrain is symbolic of the white pearls that Bahrain was famous for and the red cloth in which they were wrapped. The five serrated white points of the hoist side of the flag represent the five pillars of Islam.

National Anthem
Bahrainona

Time
GMT (Greenwich Mean Time) + 3 hours

Telephone Country Code
973

Land
A group of 35 low-lying islands in the Arabian (Persian) Gulf 24 km (14.9 miles) from the east coast of Saudi Arabia and 28 km (17.4 miles) from the western coast of Qatar

Area
711,900 sq km (274,866.1 sq miles)

Highest point
Jebel Dukhan, translated into English as the 'Mountain of Smoke' (134 m / 439.6 ft)

Climate
Mainly arid with very hot, humid summers and mild, pleasant winters

Average Monthly Temperatures in Bahrain

	Jan	Feb	Mar	Apr	May	Jun	Jul	Aug	Sep	Oct	Nov	Dec
°C	17	18	21	26	31	33	34	34	33	29	24	20
°F	62	65	70	78	87	91	94	94	91	85	76	68

Energy, minerals and bio-resources
Crude oil, crop production, electricity generation, fisheries, livestock, natural gas

Population
The estimate in 2008 was 760,168, made up of 469,553 nationals and 290,615 non-nationals.

Ethnic Groups
Bahraini Arabs (63 per cent), Asian (19 per cent), other Arabs (10 per cent), Iranian (8 per cent)

Religion
Islam (Shi'a and Sunni), Christianity (Catholics and Protestants), Baha'i, Hinduism, Parsee (Zoroastrianism), Buddhism

Languages and Dialects
Arabic, English, Farsi, Urdu

Government

Bahrain is technically a constitutional monarchy, but in fact, the king wields real power. In theory, the government of Bahrain mirrors a Western democracy with an independent legislature, judiciary and executive arm of government.

The legislature, known as the National Assembly, has two houses. Members of the Upper House, known as the Shura Council, are appointed by the king, whereas members of the Lower House, known as the Chamber of Deputies, are elected by the people. Members of the cabinet and judges are appointed by the king.

Administrative Divisions

Five governorates: Capital, Muharraq, Northern, Central and Southern.
Twelve municipalities are Gharbiyah, Hidd, Hamad, Hawar, Isa, Jidd and Haffs, Manama, Muharraq, Riffa and Janubiyah, Sharmaliyah, Sitra and Wusta

Currency

Bahraini dinars (BHD)

Agricultural Products

Fruits and vegetables

Other Products

Dairy products, fish, poultry, shrimp

Industries

Petroleum processing and refining, aluminium smelting, offshore banking, ship repairing, tourism

Exports

Aluminium, petroleum and petroleum products, textiles

Imports

Chemicals, crude oil, machinery

Port and Habours
Mina Khalifa, Mina Manama, Mina Salman, Mina Sitra

Airports
Bahrain International Airport plus three military airports

Weights and Measures
Bahrain uses the metric system with fluids measured in litres, distance in kilometres and weight measured in kilogrammes.

Bahrain pearls used to be sold per *chow* which is a local measurement of weight and gold was sold by the *tola* (weight of measeurement used in India, South Asia and the Arabian Gulf).

Acronyms
A&E	African and Eastern
ALBA	Aluminium Bahrain
ARAMCO	Arabian American Oil Company
BSTD	Bahrain Society for Training and Development
BAPCO	Bahrain Petroleum Company
BANAGAS	Bahrain National Gas Company
BHD or BD	Bahrain Dinars
BCCI	Bahrain Chamber of Commerce and Industry
BiBF	Bahrain Institute of Banking and Finance
BMA	Bahrain Monetary Agency
BATELCO	Bahrain Telecommunications Company
BDF	Bahrain Defence Force
BBA	Bahrain Businesses Association
BRTC	Bahrain Radio and Television Corporation
BMI	Bahrain Music Institute
BTF	Bahrain Tennis Federation
BPS	Bahrain Philanthropic Society
BCSR	Bahrain Centre for Study and Research
BCHR	Bahrain Centre for Human Rights
BFA	Bahrain Football Association
BMF	Bahrain Motor Federation
BSH	Bahrain Specialist Hospital
GOYS	General Organization for Youth and Sports

GOSI	General Organization for Social Insurance
(A)GCC	(Arabian) Gulf Co-Operation Council
GDN	Gulf Daily News
GARMCO	Gulf Aluminium Rolling Mill Company
GEDP	Gulf Executive Development Program
HID	Health Information Directorate
PFC	Pension Fund Commission
UAE	United Arab Emirates

Famous People

King Hamad bin Isa al Khalifa

Described by the Western press as 'young and dynamic', he became amir in 1999 on the death of his father Sheikh Isa. One of his first acts was to pardon the 200 or so anti-government detainees, give the media more freedom and invite political exiles to come home. These acts gave him an almost hero status. In 2002, he changed his title from amir to king, and in a calculated decision to gain immediate support from his subjects, decreed the forgiveness of half the debt owed by Bahrainis to the government on housing loans.

Sheikh Salman bin Hamad Al Khalifa

Crown Prince and commander-in-chief of the Bahrain Defence Force. In addition to being responsible for the security of Bahrain, he is also President of the Supreme Council of Youth and Sports and other organisations including the Alumni Club and the Bahrain Ardah (sword dancing) Society. Amongst his achievements was the initiation of an International Scholarship Scheme facilitating young Bahrainis to visit other countries in order to keep abreast of developments in the 21st century. He is also a motor sport enthusiast who personally oversaw the construction of the Formula 1 track, including the building of a spectacular main grandstand that resembles an Arab tent in an oasis of palms.

Sheikh Khalifa bin Salman Al Khalifa

Long serving head of government and prime minister since 1971. Brother of the late amir and uncle of the present king. Under his influence, Bahrain has been ranked first among

Arab and Muslim states for four consecutive years as a centre for human resource development. Sheikh Khalifa has played a key role in the economic and political development of Bahrain.

Abdullah Ali Kanoo

Chairman of the YBA Kanoo Group, a Bahrain based multinational corporation with extensive business interests. Abdullah Ali Kanoo has expanded his company by focusing on the continuous training of executives and staff, exploiting business opportunities as the AGCC countries become more integrated. He has been further developing his company's involvement in tourism to include religious travel.

James Hogan

An Australian CEO of Gulf Air, the national airline of Bahrain. At one time, the airline was in decline in terms of profitability and the number of passengers carried. Hogan turned around an airline that was losing over US$ 100 million a year and strengthened Gulf Air's balance sheet. The airline then scooped the annual award for 'Airline Turnaround of the Year' from the Centre for Asia Pacific Aviation. In 2006, James Hogan completed his tenure with Gulf Air and subsequently became CEO of Ethihad Airways in Abu Dhabi.

Places of Interest
Bahrain National Museum

Located in the northern part of Bahrain facing Muharraq city, the National Museum comprises of a 'heritage village' that reflects the architecture of Bahraini houses, buildings, streets and lanes that used to exist in the past. The architecture of the museum is based on an ancient cubic design and houses archaeological displays, artifacts of natural history and the fine arts of the Kingdom of Bahrain.

Bab Al Bahrain

This is the gateway to Bahrain and was the original building that housed government civil servants. Built in 1945, it incorporated Islamic features and is now the headquarters for the directorate of tourism. Bab Al Bahrain is a good starting point for a visit to the *souq* in Manama.

King Fahd Causeway

Opened in 1986, this 25-km (15.5-mile) causeway is one of the longest in the world and links Bahrain to Saudi Arabia. The causeway passes through Umm Na' sar Island, a sanctuary for wildlife and at the halfway mark, there is a facilities area including an observation tower with a restaurant that provides a panoramic view of Saudi Arabia.

Tree of Life

Near Jebel Dukhan, in the centre of Bahrain, is the Tree of Life. Standing alone in a barren desert, its source of water is a mystery. The flourishing acacia tree is a popular place for Bahrainis to picnic. Stone age flints have been found in the vicinity of the tree.

Bahrain Fort

There is a sign post to the right, just after Jidd Hafs roundabout on the Budaiya highway, that points the way to Bahrain Fort. The structure is a fascinating example of how forts were built. The original fort can be traced back to 2,800 BC. Excavations have uncovered treasures from many eras. Restoration has commenced on the north-east tower, and it will consist of a small museum.

Burial Mounds

Bahrain in 3000 BC was the site of the world's largest prehistoric cemetery. There are 172,000 burial mounds belonging to the Bronze Age.

Al Khamis Mosque

Located on the Shaikh Salman Road to Awali, the Al Khamis Mosque is easily identifiable by its twin minarets. The mosque is thought to be built in AD 682, one of the most ancient relics of Islam in the Arabian Gulf. The mosque has been recently restored and is protected by a perimeter wall.

Manama Souq

This is a must see. This place has a profusion of colours, sounds and aromas. Bargaining is expected and is likely to be a new shopping experience for Westerners. A visit to the gold *souq* is worthwhile as Bahrain gold is usually 21 carat and hallmarked.

Siyadi House

This is an impressive example of a 19th century building. Its fine features include ornate ceilings, stained glass windows, carved screens and a large safe set into the wall of a small upper reception room.

Museum of Pearl Diving

This is regarded as one of the most historic and important buildings in Bahrain. Its importance derives from it being the first location of the Bahrain Courts and it is a witness to the advances Bahrain has made in the application of civil law and the establishment of the Principles of Justice on solid legal foundations.

Opened in 1937, the building housed four Supreme Courts, two Religious Courts and a court hearing cases on minor estates. The building is now a heritage centre retaining the courts as they were and stands to tell the story of Bahrain, its governors and its people from the past to the present.

CULTURE QUIZ

SITUATION 1

You are an expatriate and a Bahraini family has invited you and your spouse to their house. They offer you a pre-lunch alcoholic beverage. Should you:

Ⓐ Say you don't drink alcoholic beverages but would enjoy a Pepsi or Mecca Cola?

Ⓑ Say that you would not think that it would be proper to consume an alcoholic beverage in the house of a Muslim family?

Ⓒ Say that you have a headache because you drank too much alcohol yesterday?

Ⓓ Accept the offer?

Comments

Many adult Bahraini men consume alcohol but adult Bahraini women generally do not. If the Bahraini host says he is going to consume alcohol, then it is probably OK for you and your spouse to consume alcohol. If the Bahraini host indicates that he is not going to consume alcohol, then it is generally acceptable for the husband to have one drink and better for the wife to stick to a carbonated beverage.

SITUATION 2

The Palestinian couple you met in Bahrain is visiting your country and you invite them home for dinner. You offer them a glass of beer or wine. They decline and ask if you have any Pepsi Cola. Do you:

ⓐ Serve them and yourself a glass of Pepsi Cola and return the bottle of wine you were going to have with your meal to the cellar?

ⓑ Put the bottle of wine on the table and serve yourself saying to your guests that you understand that being a Muslim they cannot consume wine but as you are a Christian the rule does not apply to you?

ⓒ Fill your glass from a bottle of wine left in the kitchen and bring it to the table without ceremony?

Comments

Alcohol is an awkward issue with Muslims. It is always a good idea to have non-alcoholic beverages available when you entertain Muslims. If they consume cola, the brand that they are most likely to consume is Pepsi Cola rather than Coca Cola. This is because Coca Cola was on the Arab boycott list for many years. **ⓐ** is a very acceptable option for your guests but not entirely necessary as you might not like to consume wine with your meal. **ⓑ** is likely to be embarrassing to your guests and shows insensitivity on your part. **ⓒ** is the best option.

SITUATION 3

You are having lunch with a Bahraini family and towards the end of the meal the wife excuses herself from the table saying it is time for her to pray, but the host stays at table and keeps talking to you. What do you do?

ⓐ Ask the Bahraini wife if you can join her saying that that this is a good opportunity for you to catch up on your Christian prayers?

ⓑ Remain at the table talking to other members of the household while the wife says her prayers?

❸ Say to the Bahraini host that this is a good time to go as you can appreciate that the family would want privacy during prayer time?

Comments

❹ is not a good idea. Even though a significant minority of Bahrainis are Christians, the two religions exist at arms length. **❹** may suggest that you are ridiculing Islam. In respect of **❸**, Muslims are not the least bit embarrassed about conducting their prayers in front of guests, strangers or whoever else is around. They do not require or expect privacy. That your host keeps talking during prayer time suggests that conversation during prayer time is acceptable, at least to him. **❸** is the best option.

SITUATION 4

You hail a taxi at the rank at Bab Al Bahrain in Manama and ask the driver the fare back to the Novotel Al Dana on Muharraq Island. He quotes you twice the price that you paid the limousine driver who brought you from the Novotel Al Dana to the post office, less than 100 m from the taxi rank. Do you:

❹ Accept the driver's quote, thinking that you got a bargain fare from the limousine driver because he was looking for a trip back to Manama?

❸ Ask the driver to turn on the meter in his taxi and say that you will pay the fare indicated when you reach the Novotel Al Dana?

❸ Negotiate a fare with the driver.

❶ Try to get another cab.

Comments

Taxis are plenty in Bahrain. Taxis have meters but drivers are often reluctant to turn them on. Most likely, you will have little chance of persuading the driver to turn on his meter. **❸** is unlikely to be achieved. If you can speak a little Arabic, you have a better chance of negotiating a better price. Your first approach would be to offer the same price as the limousine driver ❶. If unsuccessful, you are left with ❶ or ❶. Even at double the limo rate, taxi fares in Bahrain are reasonable by Western standards.

SITUATION 5

You are at the Riffa Golf Course playing with a Bahraini Muslim and you hear the call to prayer. Do you:

❶ Abandon the game?
❶ Stop playing for the duration of the prayer time?
❶ Keep playing?

Comments

Unlike Saudi Arabia, Bahraini Muslims don't have to drop everything when the call to prayer is heard. There is a grace period of up to 30 minutes before they are obliged to pray. Your Bahraini golfing partner is likely to keep playing until he finds a convenient opportunity to start praying. You wouldn't consider ❶. However, you would stop playing and wait for your partner to complete his devotions. You would not, in accordance of the etiquette of golf, keep playing. ❶ is the best option.

SITUATION 6

You are interested in learning more about Islam and a Bahraini says you should go to a mosque. Should you:

❶ Thank him for his advice and decline the offer believing that the Bahraini was only being polite and that you would not be welcomed in a mosque?
❶ Arrange to go to a mosque with the your Bahraini friend.
❶ Visit a mosque by yourself.

Comments

Some mosques in Bahrain are open to visitors from other religions. Others are closed. For example, the Ahmad Al Fateh mosque, also known as the Grand Mosque, welcomes visitors of either gender between 9:00 am and 5:00 pm except during prayer time. No prior appointment is required except for a large group of visitors. All options are available to you, but make enquiries about the particular mosque you want to visit.

SITUATION 7

You are introduced to a man wearing a white *thobe*, a black *bicht* and a red and white checked *ghoutra* with *egals*. What is his likely nationality?

A Saudi
B Palestinian
C Kuwaiti
D Omani
E Emirati
F Qatari

Comments

The least likely are **D**, **E**, **C** and **F**. Omanis and Qataris generally wear a white *ghoutra* with ends wrapped around the chin and without an *egal*. **B** is unlikely. Palestinians in Bahrain generally wear Western clothes with a black and white check *ghoutra*, if any at all. The answer is **A**, Saudi.

SITUATION 8

You have invited a Bahraini family to your house for lunch and they bring along a large box. You think it might be a gift, but is not gift-wrapped. They don't actually offer you the gift, but deposit it in a prominent position, then ignore it. Do you:

A Open the gift and offer thanks for their wonderful present.
B Thank them for the gift and keep it away to be opened later after they have departed.
C Like them, pretend that the box is not existent, and then open it later.

Comments

It is customary for the gift to be brought to the house and deposited discreetly. It is part of local culture to ignore the existence of the gift. Adopt option **C**. There is no need to acknowledge or even comment on the gift at all.

SITUATION 9

You are a Western expatriate married couple at lunch with a Bahraini, having a Bahraini-style meal. Cutlery is provided. Halfway through the meal, you or host informs you that he is going to eat with his hand (right hand only) because he can eat faster—and proceeds to do so! The hostess continues to eat with spoon and fork. How should the meal proceed from here?

A Husband and wife both eat with their hands.

B The guests follow their gender roles: the husband eats with his hand and the wife continues to use the cutlery.

C Continue eating with knife and fork.

Comments

Bahrainis, being worldly people, understand Western culinary practice, and follow it themselves when dining in restaurants, hotels and clubs. However, the head of the family sets the standards of behaviour in his own domain. Any of the options are acceptable. Do what you are most comfortable with doing.

SITUATION 10

You are an expat driver of a car involved in a collision with another car on a busy intersection. No one is injured. Both cars are slightly damaged, but drivable. Do you:

A Exchange names and insurance details and drive off.

B Call the police.

C Move the car out of the way and wait for the police to arrive.

Comments

Every accident, however minor, has to be assessed by the police. Under the law, cars cannot be moved, even if they are blocking the intersection. **B** is correct.

DO'S AND DON'TS

DO'S

- Do accept Arab coffee, tea and other non-alcoholic beverages when offered.
- Do tell Bahrainis how much you are enjoying your stay in the kingdom.
- Do dress conservatively.
- Do pronounce Bahrain as if it were two words with an emphasis on 'Bah' with a big throaty 'hhhh'.
- Do ensure that your company has a picture of the king in the foyer or a prominent place in the office.
- Do keep in touch with your country's diplomatic mission or if your country does not have a diplomatic mission, the wardens appointed by your country.
- Do bargain in the *souq*.

DON'TS

- Don't display anything that indicates you are pro-Israel or pro-Iran.
- Don't go out of your way to impress Bahrainis with your friendship.
- Don't touch a member of the opposite gender in public.
- Don't shake hands with Bahraini women unless they offer you their hand first.
- Don't discuss politics or religion.
- Don't smoke, drink or eat in public during Ramadan.
- Don't show affection or behave intimately with your spouse or partner in public.
- Don't use your left hand for eating.

GLOSSARY

NUMERALS

	Masculine	Feminine
zero	*sifr*	*sifr*
one	*waahid*	*wahdah*
two	*ithnain*	*thintain*
three	*thalaat*	*thalaathah*
four	*arba'*	*arba'ah*
five	*khams*	*khamsah*
six	*sitt*	*sittah*
seven	*sab'*	*sab'ah*
eight	*thamaan*	*thamaaniah*
nine	*tisi'*	*tis'ah*
ten	*'ashr*	*'ashrah*

PRONOUNS

ana	I
inta	you (masculine)
inti	you (female)
huwa	he or it
hiya	she or it
ihna	we
intuu	you (plural)
hum	they

SHOPPING

walad	boy
khubbis	bread

sayyaarah	car
gahwah	coffee
sharikah	company
bint	daughter
yaum	day
sharab	drink
akal	eat
samak	fish
sadiij	friend
bustaan	garden
bint	girl
zain	good
khaliij	gulf
ra:s	head
haarr	hot
saa'ah	hour
bait	house
saghiir	little
shway shway	little by little
shuuf	look
yimkin	maybe
haliib	milk
fuluus	money
umm	mother
jebel	mountain
laazim	necessary
laa	no
shimaal	north
minfaDlak	please
'aish	rice
saghiir	small

USEFUL PHRASES
Greetings

First person	*Salaam alaikum* (Peace be upon you)
Second person	*Wa-alaikum as-salam* (And upon you peace)
First person	*Sabah al-khair* (Good morning)
Second person	*Sabah an-nuur* (Good morning)
First person	*Kaif haalak* (How are you?—literally meaning, 'how is your colour?')
Second person	*Al-hamdu llillah* (Praise be to God)
First person	*Fii amaan illah* (Goodbye—literally meaning, 'may God go with you')
Second person	*Fii amaan il karim* (Goodbye—literally meaning, 'may God go with you')

Conversation

First person	*Ana maa shuftak min* (I have not seen you for a long time.)
Second person	*Aish taguul ana maa faham* (What did you say? I did not understand.)
First person	*Ana mit:assif, ana nasiit ismak aish ismak, minfaDlak* (I am sorry, I have forgotten your name. What is your name?)
Second person	*Ismii Ahmad* (My name is Ahmad.)

First person	*Tarrid shaay aw gahwah*
	(Would you like coffee or tea?)
Second person	*Kulluh waahid*
	(It's all the same to me.)
First person	*Wain bilaadak*
	(Where is your home?)
Second person	*Ana min al-Hid*
	(I am from Hidd)
First person	*Titkallan ingiliizi*
	(Do you speak English?)
Second person	*Shway bass*
	(Only a little.)
First person	*Wain tashugl*
	(Where do you work?)
Second person	*Ana taajir fis-sung*
	(I am a merchant in the market.)

RESOURCE GUIDE

EMERGENCY NUMBERS

There is only one emergency telephone number 999. By dialing 999, you can be connected to all the emergency services including ambulance, fire brigade and the police. There are separate telephone numbers for major hospitals and pharmacies.

- Ambulance, fire, police **999**

MAKING LOCAL AND INTERNATIONAL PHONE CALLS

Bahrain's phone system is provided by the Bahrain Telecommunication Company (BATELCO) that was established in 1981. Land lines cover nearly all residences and businesses. There is a mobile phone network with 30 base stations. BATELCO has public pay phones that can be operated by coin, phone cards and credit cards. They are few and far between but have been sighted by the authors at shopping malls. Pay phones are not well patronised.

INTERNET FACILITIES

Internet connections are widely available through Speednet, a superior Internet access service based on Asynchronous Digital Subscriber Line (ADSL).

HOSPITALS

Hospitals in Bahrain deliver high quality medical services, which are usually free to Bahrainis and non-Bahrainis working for the government. There is also an electronic medical library where health professionals can have access to the latest medical research, drug information and patient educational resources. Hospitals invite international specialists to perform surgery and give lectures to increase the expertise of Bahraini doctors.

The following are a list of reputable hospitals. Please check the local listings for the current telephone numbers.

- Al Sulmaniah Medical Complex (SMC)
- American Mission Hospital
- Awali Hospital
- Bahrain Defence Force Hospital (BDF)
- Bahrain Specialist Hospital (BSH)
- Gulf Dental Hospital
- IBN Al Nafees Hospital
- International Hospital of Bahrain
- King Hamad Hospital

SCHOOLS

Western expats either send their children to a school back in their own country or a non-government school in Bahrain. Usually, they will send their children to the Bahrain American School or St Christopher's which provide primary and secondary education. St Christopher's teaches a British syllabus and has high academic standards, often requiring students to pass an entrance exam.

There are a number of schools including Sacred Heart School, Pakistan URDU School, The Asian School, The Indian School and the New Indian School catering to the needs of expats from the sub-continent and Asia.

Please check the local listings for the most current telephone number.

Language Schools

- Ecole Francais de Bahrain
- American Cultural and Educational Centre
- Berlitz Bahrain
- The British Council

International Schools

- St Christopher's
- British School of Bahrain
- Bahrain American (International) School
- Indian School Of Bahrain
- Montessori School
- Philippine School
- The Asian School

EXPAT CLUBS

There are a number of clubs catering to the needs of guest workers and their families. Some clubs like the British Club and the Indian Club meet the needs of expats from specific countries. Other clubs like the Riffa Golf Club, the Bahrain Rugby Club and the Bahrain Yacht Club meet the needs of expats who like to play specific sports. There are also clubs like the BAPCO Club for employees of specific companies.

- Awali Golf Club
- Al Ahli Club
- Bahrain Tennis Club
- Bahrain Rugby Football Club
- Bahrain Yacht Club
- BAPCO Club
- Indian Club
- Riffa Golf Club
- The Equestrian and Horse Racing Club
- British Club
- Dilmun Club
- Tamil Cultural Association

RELIGIOUS INSTITUTIONS

Religious institutions that can be visited by non-Muslim people include the Ahmed Al Fateh Mosque (Grand Mosque) outside prayer time, the Saar Islamic Centre Mosque by appointment and Beit Al Quran at selected times.

For such a small country whose population is mainly Muslim, St Christopher's Cathedral is the joint spiritual home to the Anglican Bishop of Cyprus and the Gulf. Christian churches include St Christopher's Cathedral and the Sacred Heart Church. Both hold church services on Sundays although the greatest congregations are present at their Friday services as this is a holiday for most people. Other Christian denominations are represented in Bahrain as are other faiths.

VOLUNTEER ORGANISATIONS

For expats wanting to participate in volunteer work, there are a number of opportunities. They include the Bahrain Society for the Prevention of Cruelty to Animals (BSPCA), which operates a thrift shop, Helpline which provides a 24-hour telephone service to listen and help people during their hour of need and the Indian Ladies Association (ILA) which has a charity card scheme.

- Indian Ladies Association (ILA)
- The Lions club
- Bahrain Society for the Prevention of Cruelty to Animals (BSCPA)

BOOKSHOPS

Most bookshops are attached to five-star and four-star hotels. They include:

- Crown Plaza
- Delmon International Hotel
- Gulf Hotel
- Hilton
- Novotel Al Dana
- Ramada Hotel Bahrain
- Regency InterContinental
- The Diplomat Radisson SAS
- Sheraton Bahrain Hotel
- The Ritz Carlton

Others include:

- Family Bookshop
- Bookshop at Tourism office at Bab Al Bahrain
- Bookshop at Bahrain National Museum

NEWSPAPERS/ MAGAZINES

Bahrain has two daily newspapers printed in English and two daily newspapers printed in Arabic. No magazines are printed in Bahrain other than government publications.

Newspapers:

- *Akbar Alkhaleej*
- *Al Ayam*
- *Bahrain Tribune*
- *Gulf Daily News*

DIPLOMATIC MISSIONS

Many countries have embassies, a consulate general or other forms of diplomatic mission in Bahrain. Some countries like Australia have an ambassador accredited to Bahrain but are residents in another country, such as Saudi Arabia.

List of diplomatic missions in Bahrain include:

- Algeria
- Bangladesh
- Belgium
- Britain
- China
- Cyprus
- Denmark
- Egypt
- France
- Germany
- Greece
- Indian
- Iran
- Iraq
- Japan
- Jordan
- Korea
- Kuwait
- Lebanon
- Morocco
- Netherlands
- Norway
- Oman
- Pakistan
- Palestine
- Philippines
- Portugal
- Russia
- Saudi Arabia
- Sweden
- Switzerland
- Taiwan
- Tunisia
- Turkey
- United States
- Yemen

WEBSITES
General Information
CIA Factbook on Bahrain
http://www.odci.gov/cia/publications/factbook/geos/ba.html

The Bahrain Government
www.bahrain.gov.bh

Visa and Travel Information
British Embassy in Bahrain
www.ukembassy.gov.bh

US Department of State:
- Bureau of Consular Affairs
  http://travel.state.gov

- Bahrain Embassy in the United States
  www.bahrainembassy.org

Tourist information
US Department of State
www.state.gov/g/drl/rls/hrrrt/2002/18288.htm

Lonely Planet Guide
http://www.lonelyplanet.com/destinations/middle_east/
bahrain

Gulf Air
http://www.gulfairco.com

Tourism in Bahrain
www.bahraintourism.com

History of Bahrain
http://www.middleeast.com/bahrain.htm

Islamic Culture
http://www.zawaj.com/links.html

Middle East Customs and Gestures
Defence Languages Institute: World Religion & Culture
http://wrc.lingnet.org/mec.htm

Employment
http://www.middleeastnews.com/bahrainjobopp.html
http://www.egyrec.com/bahrain/
http://www.escapeartist.com/bahrain/jobs.htm

Business in Bahrain
Bahrain Chamber of Commerce
http://www.commerce.gov.bh/english

FURTHER READING

There is hardly ever a day when a Middle Eastern news story is not written into a plethora of books. This random selection of further reading rounds out some of the issues discussed in *CultureShock! Bahrain*.

HISTORY OF BAHRAIN

Personal Column: The History of Bahrain as a British Protectorate and Part of the Indian Empire. Charles Belgrave. Hutchinson & Co. Ltd, 1960.

- Charles Belgrave, as advisor to the rulers of Bahrain, played a key role in developing Bahrain as the principal centre amongst the Arabian Gulf sheikhdoms. Bahrainis now believe that the kingdom has moved on and is being driven by the vision of the king, prime minister and the principal merchants.

BOOKS ON THE ISLAMIC RELIGION

The World from Islam: A Journey of Discovery through the Muslim heartland. George Negus. Harper Collins, 2003.

- These days, the less informed in the Western world see every Muslim as a potential terrorist. This book tells that most Muslims in the Middle East including Bahrain and the Arabian Gulf are law-abiding people tolerant of other religions who just want to get on with their lives and be free of the conflicts in the region.

BOOKS ON ETIQUETTE

Don't They Know its Friday? Cross Cultural Considerations for Business and Life in the Gulf. Jeremy Williams. Motivate Publishing, 1999.

- A light-hearted, amusing but practical guide to how business is done in the Arabian Gulf, including Bahrain. Some Western expat academics holding teaching posts at Arabian Gulf Universities have said it is a bit over the top but very readable.

The Saudis: Inside the Desert Kingdom. Sandra Mackey. W.W. Norton, 2002.

- A book about Bahrain's big brother and nearest neighbour, the desert kingdom of Saudi Arabia. Living in Saudi Arabia as the dependent wife of an American doctor, Sandra Mckay led a clandestine life as an undergraduate journalist reporting on events and analysing the forces that will shape the kingdom's future. Although the book is a little dated, much of its contents remain valid today.

ABOUT THE AUTHORS

Harvey Tripp is a graduate of the University of Melbourne, Australia and attended primary school in Bahrain. He spent most of his corporate life in international business—holding senior management positions in major international consumer goods companies, including the management of their operations in Bahrain. Harvey has lectured on international business including topics such as how to do business in the Arabian Gulf at a number of Universities in Australia. He has also sat on the advisory boards of universities and other tertiary institutions to help develop their international business programmes. Harvey has been a consultant to small and medium sized businesses and has had interim executive assignments with corporations whose primary focus is international business. He has also been a director of small and medium sized Australian companies. He is the co-author of *Culture Shock! Success Secrets to Maximise Business in Hong Kong*, *Culture Shock! Success Secrets to Maximise Business in the United Arab Emirates* and *Culture Shock! A Guide to Customs and Etiquette Saudi Arabia*.

Margaret Tripp, a graduate of Deakin University, recently retired as a senior teacher at a leading high school in Australia focusing on the attraction of overseas students. Margaret has travelled extensively throughout the Middle East including Bahrain and has met with a wide variety of decision-makers, both Bahrainis and expats who make up the community. She has a sound understanding of the cultural aspects of life in Bahrain, including the role of women at home and in the workforce. Margaret has been a board member of a small to medium sized Australian company. She co-authored *Culture Shock! Success Secrets to Maximise Business in Hong Kong* and *Culture Shock! Success Secrets to Maximise Business in the United Arab Emirates*.

INDEX

Titles in the CultureShock! series:

Argentina	France	Russia
Australia	Germany	San Francisco
Austria	Hawaii	Saudi Arabia
Bahrain	Hong Kong	Scotland
Beijing	Hungary	Shanghai
Belgium	India	Singapore
Bolivia	Ireland	South Africa
Borneo	Italy	Spain
Brazil	Jakarta	Sri Lanka
Britain	Japan	Sweden
Bulgaria	Korea	Switzerland
Cambodia	Laos	Syria
Canada	London	Taiwan
Chicago	Malaysia	Thailand
Chile	Mauritius	Tokyo
China	Morocco	Turkey
Costa Rica	Munich	United Arab
Cuba	Myanmar	Emirates
Czech Republic	Netherlands	USA
Denmark	New Zealand	Vancouver
Ecuador	Paris	Venezuela
Egypt	Philippines	
Finland	Portugal	

For more information about any of these titles, please contact any of our Marshall Cavendish offices around the world (listed on page ii) or visit our website at:

www.marshallcavendish.com/genref